Issues in Higher Education
and Economic Development

American Association
of State Colleges and Universities

©1986 by American Association of State Colleges and Universities
Washington, D.C.

Library of Congress Cataloging-in-Publication Data

Issues in higher education and economic development.

    1.Economic development—Effect of education on—
Congresses. 2.Education—Economic aspects—United
States—Congresses. 3.Science and industry—United
States—Congresses. I.American Association of State
Colleges and Universities.
HD75.7.R43   1986   338.9 86-20680
ISBN 0-88044-079-1

Contents

Introduction   v

Economic Trends: Impact On Higher Education

1. Maintaining the Nation's Competitive Edge   3
   Juanita Kreps
2. Business and Higher Education: Imperative to Adapt   11
   Pat Choate
3. Developing Inner-City Business   19
   James Howell
4. Transferring Technologies to Industry   23
   David Swanson
5. State Initiatives in Economic Development: Four Successful Strategies   35
   Charles Bartsch

An International Perspective

6. Developing International Trade at the Local Level   43
   Andrew Young
7. Bringing Colorado Products to the World Market   51
   Patty Martillaro
8. Pleasures and Pitfalls in Developing International Trade   57
   Frank Hoy

The Higher Education Mission and Economic Development

9. A Policy Environment for Human Capital Development   63
   Peter Smith
10. The Responsibilities of Public Universities for Economic Development   73
    Thomas Stauffer
11. Higher Education and Economic Development: A Symbiotic Relationship   81
    Wade Gilley
12. The Power of the People in Community Economic Development   89
    Catherine Rolzinski

Institutional Policies and Economic Development Programs

13. Universities, Centers, and Economic Development: Converting Rhetoric to Reality   99
    Marshall Kaplan
14. Establishing an Effective, University-Based Technical Assistance Program   109
    Karl Turner
15. Encouraging Faculty Involvement in University Economic Development Programs   117
    Patricia Crosson
16. University Management of Intellectual Property   129
    Radford King
17. Linking Universities with Communities: The Cleveland Experience   137
    John Flower

Appendix

National Project on Higher Education and Economic Development   147

Introduction

Higher education institutions in the United States constitute the single most significant resource that can influence economic development. They provide education and training that expand our human capital. They conduct basic and applied research that generate new technologies, new products, and new services. And they share the knowledge resources and the expertise that help transfer innovations from sector to sector and help American business maintain a competitive edge.

Every sector of higher education, and every type of institution, plays one or more of these roles. Two-year, four-year, and graduate institutions; public and private colleges and universities; all have an economic impact ranging from their communities and regions to the international market place. More than ever, state policy makers, local government officials, business and labor leaders, and community groups are looking to colleges and universities for assistance in facing economic development problems.

Problems in and potentials for the effective involvement of colleges and universities in economic development are explored in this book. The issues were identified by a group of advisors—experts in the areas of university-based economic development programs, labor and management studies, and state and national policy initiatives. (See Appendix.) This group of advisors was convened in conjunction with a national project on higher education and economic development conducted during 1985 and 1986 by the American Association of State Colleges and Universities (AASCU) in cooperation with the National Association of Management and Technical Assistance Centers (NAMTAC). The purpose of the project was to identify program models that effectively connect higher education resources to economic development needs, and to alert higher education leaders to the potential for economic impact contained within their own institutions.

Our authors grapple with the difficult questions that arise when academic institutions become engaged with the profit-making sector: Who should take the initiative for economic development? What is the proper role for a higher education institution? Does university intervention give one business an unfair advantage over another? Who owns knowledge? How can faculty members be rewarded for sharing their expertise, without being lured away from higher education by the larger salaries in business and industry? What policies enhance effective collaboration between higher education and business? How can the needs and goals of the community best be incorporated in planning for economic development? Readers will discover that colleges and universities across the country are trying to address these issues, and many promising approaches have been developed.

The articles in this book are based on presentations at the National Conference on Higher Education and Economic Development held in Atlanta, Georgia, April 1986, and cosponsored by AASCU, NAMTAC, the American Council on Education, the Association of Urban Universities, the Council of Independent Colleges, the Federal Laboratory Consortium for Technology Transfer, the International City Management Association, the National Association of State Universities and Land-Grant Colleges, the Northeast-Midwest Institute, and SRI International. Nearly 200 college and university administrators and faculty members, government officials, and business leaders attended the conference.

This book of readings is a companion to *The Higher Education—Economic Development Connection*, a study conducted for AASCU by SRI International and published earlier in 1986. Both volumes and the national conference were made possible by a grant from the U.S. Department of Commerce, Economic Development Administration, under the National Technical Assistance Program.

AASCU takes a leadership role in encouraging economic development initiatives by public colleges and universities. The association's Task Force on Economic Development is made up of presidents and chancellors of member institutions representing the Committees on Science and Technology, Urban Affairs, Corporate/College Relations, and Agriculture, Renewable Resources and Rural Development. (See Appendix.) In 1985 the task force conducted a survey to collect information on existing economic development programs at public, four-year colleges and universities, and started a computer-based clearinghouse. The task force is currently developing a mission statement that connects the university's traditional roles in teaching, research, and public service, with new and emerging needs in regional and state economic development. The Office of Community Development and Public Service is the organizational unit within the association that relates to the public-service programs and activities state colleges and universities provide in response to the needs of the communities and regions they serve.

Helen Roberts, Director
Office of Community Development and Public Service
American Association of State Colleges and Universities

Economic Trends:
Impact on Higher
Education

1

Maintaining the Nation's Competitiveness

Juanita Kreps

The author is a former United States Secretary of Commerce.

Human capital, defined as the skill, dexterity and knowledge of the population, has become the critical input that determines the rate of growth of the economy and the well-being of the population.
—Eli Ginzberg and George J. Vojta, *Scientific American*, March 1981

Any discussion of higher education and economic development must begin with an examination of the dramatic, nationwide transformation now underway: the shift from an industrial to an information society. The changes now overtaking us call for careful appraisal of education's capacity to meet the new challenges. Can higher education do a better job of directing the teaching and research talents of its educators to the issues the nation faces in an internationalized, highly competitive economy?

This is not the first time education has been asked to respond to changing economics. As George Autry points out, land-grant colleges helped the nation through the agricultural revolution. Today's colleges and universities are being looked to for guidance during an even more pervasive transition. The need for their response is urgent, for without the thoughtful contributions of scholars and teachers, the nation's productivity will decline, its standard of living suffer, and its world leadership diminish.

In analyzing economic changes, economists often tend to dwell on cyclical trends, as measured by month-to-month shifts in unemployment, inflation, and interest rates. But educators can take the longer view, probing forces that will reshape our lives far into the future. Two significant forces have been the internationalization of the economy (including the global competition it has generated) and the quickening march of technology.

A global economy

Nothing is as obvious yet as overlooked as the fact that we no longer have a "U.S. economy." What we have is a huge market place—by far, the world's richest—that exchanges goods, services, capital and, increasingly, information, from all over the world. American consumers buy clothing from Taiwan as easily as they buy vegetables from a farm in the next county. The Japanese not only sell us automobiles manufactured on their shores but open plants in our country to be supplied with components made elsewhere. Our own multinational firms that have traditionally employed a large proportion of American job seekers are increasing their investments and locating more of their factories abroad. And the biggest player of all, the U.S. Treasury, is now financing much of its debt in foreign markets, drawing into this country about a hundred billion dollars a year of savings that our own citizens do not supply.

None of us is oblivious to the global nature of today's markets. Yet we continue to underestimate the level of change such internationalization produces, and we often persist in discussing economic policy as if our nation still had an isolated economy. One hears, for example, the admonition that until we put our own economy in order we cannot deal with disturbing international developments—as if the two sets of problems could be separated.

Our failure to think in global terms, and the ensuing lag of policy behind commerical practice, leads us to do, in the words of Ken Galbraith, "many things that are unnecessary, some that are unwise, and a few that are insane."

An internationalized economy forces us to reckon with the worldwide impact of our domestic policies. Just as we cannot contain scientific knowledge of technical advances within our borders, neither can we limit the effect of our fiscal and monetary policies to purely domestic events.

Our tax decisions affect all markets. A change in U.S. spending patterns can change the economic outlook in other leading nations as well as developing countries. Similarly, economic developments in this country largely reflect policies pursued by other governments and foreign businesses. On the formation of those policies Americans have little say.

The economic vulnerability we Americans now feel stems chiefly from this internationalization process, which limits the control we can exercise at home while increasing the impact of our policies abroad. All nations are caught in the same economic net. For illustration, one has only to recall the oil shortages of the early and late seventies, which placed critical restrictions on growth throughout the world and brought the United States its highest rate of inflation in modern times. In terms of losses in jobs and real incomes, of industrial dislocations, and even of social instability, the damage was enormous. Yet energy-importing countries could do little in the short run to mitigate these effects.

Currently, the fall in oil prices is destabilizing to the oil-producing states and countries, and to other countries throughout the world. Of course, it has also boosted U.S. markets. But there is little doubt that this trend will be reversed in the future, as oil exploration declines and shortages threaten once again.

What have these changes meant in terms of our nation's competitive position in the world?

A few years ago, when IBM and the FBI charged employees of two Japanese firms with stealing computer secrets from IBM, Americans did not know whether to laugh or cry—cry because this seemingly absurd attempt was one more blow to U.S./Japanese relations, or laugh at the notion that the highly productive Japanese, whose trade surplus even then was running about $20 billion, would need any of our commercial know-how. The incident also led to nostalgic thoughts of that strikingly different era following World War II, when our technology, the envy of the world, was avidly sought by industrialized nations and the demand for American-made goods was unparalleled.

The global competition that began in earnest in the early 1970s seemed to take much of American industry by surprise. Japan and other newly industrialized countries, primarily in the Pacific basin, adopted aggressive strategies to capture world markets for their exports. The volume of world trade has since grown rapidly, and today more than 70 percent of our products must compete with foreign-made goods.

The price of our currency has compounded the problem. The 50-percent rise in the value of the dollar during the first half of the 1980s made our exports more expensive and our imports cheaper, which helped create a $148-billion deficit for 1985. The expensive dollar further weakened our competitive position in agriculture, mineral resources, and manufacturing. In the case of manufacturing, the high-priced American dollar and low labor costs in developing countries have increased the march of U.S. plants to foreign countries. This "exporting of jobs," when combined with ever-rising imports, has led to strong sentiment favoring protectionist legislation.

Technology's ambivalent consequences

While international developments redefined trade patterns, new technologies improved productivity by substituting capital for labor, transmitting information around the world, and providing scientific and technical breakthroughs that revolutionized the market place.

We have seen the commercialization of an array of microelectronics and information technologies. The use of computers in virtually every office and factory has both revitalized older industries and created new ones. Other technologies are approaching commercialization: biotechnologies, health and medical technologies, new materials and new breakthroughs in communications.

Because of worldwide market forces and improvements in efficiency, all institutions have to adapt to harsh new realities. Only by learning to meet the world's tests can we avoid losing our markets and our jobs. We could try to rely more heavily on protectionism, but in the long run we must find ways to apply our advanced technology and to invest more heavily in human resources. Otherwise, we shall lose the economic growth we have long enjoyed and forfeit a leadership role in world affairs.

As we turn these new developments to our advantage, the effect will be enormously beneficial, not just to ourselves but to the peoples around the globe. We can expand productive capacity, improve our research capacities, and improve information sharing and problem solving in a wide range of issues. The potential for material progress is vast, and with such progress comes greatly enhanced health and well-being.

The promise is clear. What is not at all clear are the policies and programs we need to develop in order to ensure these gains. Our record to date has been spotty. Faced with two threats—the loss of markets to foreign producers and the loss of jobs to foreign workers and automation—public policy has been confused and contradictory. In this country we have suffered losses on both fronts.

What we have tried

We have tried almost everything. We have protected some industries from excessive imports, paying higher prices for goods in order to save jobs and incomes. These actions are not without merit. Removing all limits to the import of textiles, for example, would quickly jeopardize an industry that is job intensive, with the bulk of the jobs going to low-skilled persons for whom alternatives are now quite bleak. Their job prospects can be improved in the future only if the public is willing to devote the necessary resources to raise their education and skill levels.

We have tried to negotiate better foreign markets for our own products. In particular, we have argued for better access to Japanese markets, pointing out their $50-billion trade surplus with the U.S., but to no avail. Their traditional motive for trade has not been to increase their total supply of goods or services for consumption, but to guarantee economic self-sufficiency. Moreover, their system of targeting new markets to conquer and then providing governmental support for those efforts has been very successful. We not only do not trust our government to pick the winners—relying instead on market forces that have served us well in the past—but we follow policies that undermine the ability of American firms to compete with their foreign counterparts.

We have tried talking the dollar down, with some success, but the effects are short-lived. We have provided tax incentives for investment in capital goods, reasoning that industry needs to spend more for the latest technology in order to lower costs. Again, policy has helped, though not enough to offset the low labor rates in Korea, Brazil, Taiwan, and many other newly industrialized nations.

What we have not tried

We have not tried often enough to meet the clear need for additional educational resources to address these problems. We have not, as a nation, provided sufficient resources to educate the youth who will have to find jobs in the new environment, or the middle-aged who are being displaced by the forces of technology and world competition. Nor have we been willing to direct enough research funds to universities to stimulate the necessary scientific discovery and its application.

Granted, private industry has developed liaisons with research institutions. But far too little attention has been given to governmentally sponsored programs, particularly at the federal level, that would utilize the research and teaching capacities of educators.

Lack of attention to this approach is puzzling in view of two developments: first, the widely recognized need for better basic and technical education, given the greater complexity of future jobs; second, the opportunities to tap higher education's facilities and expertise at a time when the numbers of youth of usual college age are declining. Seldom has a critical national problem been accompanied by a more promising set of resources for its solution. Ray Marshall, former Secretary of Labor and long-time advocate of greater investments in education, noted recently that "it's the eve of an internationalized information society, and the principal need is for improving learning skills and education at all levels, but especially in technology levels below engineering. Communication and interpersonal skills will be almost as important."

There are, of course, many programs underway. The recent AASCU book, *The Higher Education—Economic Development Connection: Emerging Roles for Public Colleges and Universities in a Changing Economy,* details the work in progress nationwide, including a variety of institutional models. It should thus not be difficult to identify the processes that work and to pinpoint the impediments we must remove in order to move ahead.

In devising various strategies for becoming more fully involved in economic development, the higher education community should start by thinking in quite broad terms. Its challenge at this point is to lay out a range of options for colleges and universities, enabling different institutions to develop different formats. Some broad guidelines should also be established to give a degree of cohesion to the overall effort and to provide a structure whereby institutions can pool their experiences and ideas in the future. Most of all, the community should press for greater attention and more public funds for the nations' economic development needs, particularly in the areas of teaching and research.

The challenge: more research, better teaching

First, as stated previously, different institutions have different capabilities.

Graduate universities need to concentrate on research that will improve technology and accelerate implementation throughout the private and public sectors. If the nation continues to lose competitive advantage in the highly complex and advanced technologies, it shall lose its manufacturing sector to other parts of the world. The greatest single pool of creative talent is the university faculty, whose research is underfunded and often focused on objectives unrelated to the need for improvements in commercially related technology. (Witness the imbalance between funding for the defense establishment and that devoted to broadly based scientific discovery.)

To both universities and four-year colleges falls the responsibility of teaching what today's youth need to know in order to become productive in the global market place. Clearly, we have not been keeping up with other nations, where both educational emphasis and resources are directed toward the technical demands of today's job market. As Ray Marshall points out, new knowledge is required by the pervasiveness of the technology. Flexibility and broadly based skills will be necessary because of the rapid changes and displacements throughout the labor force and the professions, because production will be "more coordinated and collective," tomorrow's graduates will also need more communicating and interpersonal skills. Increasingly, Marshall concludes, the information world will reward people for what they know rather than what they do.

In short, it is important to remember that the teaching that best serves our economic development goals does not call for new literature, but rather for teaching the basic skills that enable students to interpret the instructions that accompany most of today's jobs. Although this level of teaching is generally the province of primary and secondary schools, the fact that it is often poorly done should challenge research-minded professors in a wide range of disciplines: education, psychology, sociology, political science, economics, mathematics.

The need for improved instruction at the college level should not be overlooked. In *Megatrends,* John Naisbitt argues that "to attract and keep high-tech industry, states must be prepared to supply a steady stream of college graduates with the technological sophistication required to keep abreast of development in their fields."

The need for better instruction was recently lamented by Labor Secretary Brock, who said, "We are building a huge glob of permanently unemployed that's going to bubble up through the demographic charts for the next 30 years—people who lack the education and skill to hold any job. They number in the high hundreds of thousands at the moment, but it will be in the low millions in the near term. This is an absolute insanity for them, and for us."

Despite some lethargy in the educational system and the obvious need for additional resources, colleges and universities are increasingly recognized as key players in the nation's race to keep up with changing economics. As late as a decade ago, much less attention was given to the impending shortage of skills and less still to the role higher education could play in the solution.

Today there is a growing appreciation of the need to invest more heavily in human resources. So far, it is mainly talk. But it is important talk. David Birch of MIT speaks of the "thoughtware" sector of the next 10-15 years, pointing out that "it doesn't require power, energy, transportation, coal. It requires brains. That's the major resource. If you look at where small businesses are growing . . . in the United States, they are, to an extraordinary extent, concentrated around centers of higher education and learning that are of higher [quality]."

His study shows that of the top twelve factors influencing the regional location of high-tech companies, the availability of labor skills ranked first and the existence of academic institutions fourth. (Labor costs and tax climate were the other factors among the top four.)

The centrality of higher education has not been lost on political leaders. According to Governor Lamm of Colorado, "There is a raw material in the new industrial order that is taking precedence over coal and iron. That raw material is education. In a real sense, the education of today is the economy of tomorrow."

One other example of the improved national climate: The Education Commission of the States, chaired by former Governor of North Carolina, James B. Hunt, created a National Task Force on Education for Economic Growth. The Task Force points out that

> In the United States today, colleges and universities are called upon to perform two vital missions prerequisite to technological innovation: educating the professional workforce of tomorrow, and providing a strong and expanding research base for the nation's economy. Both functions are absolutely essential to the innovative process. Research provides the new knowledge on which innovative processes are based, and education sharpens the creative minds which will envision and shape tomorrow's advances.

What does all the talk mean? How significant is the improved climate, with its increasingly realistic view of the nations' educational needs?

Our optimism must be tempered by the impact that current budget-cutting legislation is bound to have. Future availability of federal funds for state programs, education or otherwise, is going to be limited, and states may be forced to shift budget lines or raise taxes for education. But the case for educational efforts on behalf of economic development could assume a much higher priority. Moreover, reduced student enrollments may free up public resources. Private funds, too, are available. Corporations are making large grants of money and equipment to colleges and universities for teaching and research.

If our nation is to offer its youth a world-class education, we must recognize that it will be expensive, that it will require a major allocation of public and private dollars, and that it mandates attention to high standards of achievement we have not always maintained.

The benefits are undisputed, however. "Human resource development pays high dividends," Ray Marshall argues, "and it will be very costly to the individual welfare of Americans and our national economic and political power if we fail to make these investments."

2

Business and Higher Education: Imperative to Adapt

Pat Choate

The author is director of TRW's Office of Policy Analysis, in which he studies long-term U.S. competitiveness.

History teaches that when nations fail to adapt, they decline. When we look back at Rome, Greece, Imperial Spain, and Britain, we see that each had its moment in the sun, its glory, and then faded from view. Historian J. H. Elliot captured the essence of the dilemma in his epitaph for Imperial Spain: "At their moment of crisis they were unwilling to surrender their memories, nor to alter the antique patterns of their lives, for they had lost the essential ingredient for survival, the willingness to change." In a very real sense, the United States has reached a moment of crisis.

When we look across the economic spectrum, we find that in one industry after another, American firms are losing their position in the global market place. The trend began with industries like apparel and textiles and spread to consumer electronics. It has afflicted steel, automobiles and, now, our most advanced industries—computers, biotechnology, semiconductors, pharmaceuticals. It soon will affect aircraft production and a diversity of other industries that undergird this economy, that provide jobs, that produce the wealth and income on which most of our national programs, our national aspirations, are grounded and financed.

The need for flexibility

The question we face as a nation is, first, why is this happening, and more important, what can we do about it? The "why" is rather staightforward. We find ourselves caught at the convergence of two great historic trends. One was well described a half century ago by Joseph Shumpeter, the Austrian economist at Harvard. He said that the processes of capitalism in themselves were a matter of creative destruction, a process of endless change in which the old is incessantly driven out by the new, where new technology, new goods, new services, new forms of communication and transportation, new markets, new competitors were altering the economic structure from within. The second trend has been described by historian Edward Gibbons, by economists such as Thorstein Veblen, Clarence Ayers, and more recently, Mangor Olsen, who have made the point that as societies age, they become less flexible, less willing to adapt.

The "why" of our economic dilemma is contained in the confrontation between these two trends. The processes of creative destruction described by Shumpeter are today ever more present. The processes of change are fast and accelerating. Their scope, which has always been wide, is broadening. American control over that change, which has always been weak, is lessening. And by the same token, as our society and our institutions have aged, they have begun to ossify. What we find at the root of most of our economic problems is the convergence of those two accelerating forces: broadening change and a slower ability to adapt, a growing and pervasive inflexibility.

Two schools of economic change

There are two ways to address these problems. One I call the "Damon Runyon school of economic change"; the other I call the "Mae West school of economic change." The Damon Runyon school is based on his famous observation about going to the racetrack: "The race may not always go to the strong and to the swift, but that's how to bet your money." The Mae West school is based on her observation that "if something is worth doing well, it's worth doing very slowly." I personally am in the Damon Runyon school of economics.

The challenge we face, then, is how to be swift and strong. We must recognize that, while we have suffered serious reverses over the past several years, at the same time we face the future with formidable strengths by any measure. We still have the world's largest capital base. We still have the world's greatest research and development structure. We still generally have the world's best technology and certainly the capacity to create a great deal more. We have a great educational network in place, and in general we still have the world's most productive, skilled, and educated work force.

The problem, however, is that because of our inflexiblity, these assets are not the strengths they could be because we are not applying them well. The challenge we face for business, for education, for government, and for the general citizenry is to find out what is keeping us from deploying those assets and resources. The starting point is first to recognize some of the changes we are going to face.

A prelude to the future

One of the changes we will face is in technology. It's a force of change that's radically altering work and life here and abroad. We know that the changes we've seen in the past are probably just a prelude to what is coming. One simple reason we know that is the fact that 90 percent of all the scientists and engineers who have ever lived are alive and at work today. That sets the basis for rapid change. Put another way, most of us were alive when the first computer was put in place in 1946. Think about the differences computers have made from then to now. We are going to have even greater advances in the future. That means that work is going to shift between here and abroad, and the nature of work is going to alter radically. We can expect that most individuals, because of technological shifts coupled with changes in trade, will be forced to change occupations three times, and jobs six to seven times, during their careers.

By the same token, if we can remain technologically advanced, we can create enough good jobs, we can create enough markets, we can use our economic position to provide work, wealth, and income.

The second driving force of change with which we've yet to grapple fully is trade. The United States economy in only twenty-five years has changed from closed to open. Where we were once economically independent, we now are economically interdependent. We once had a little less than 9 percent of our gross national product consumed in trade; now it's about 25 percent, and we're probably going to wind up in the 1990s with one-third of our GNP in global trade.

If we were to take that part of our GNP that is trade, pull it out, and make it a separate economy, it would be the fifth largest in the world. Therefore, given that size, given its influence in the world, we cannot close our markets. We cannot go back to an isolated economy. We are deeply and irreversibly engaged in the global economy. About 70 percent of our industries now face foreign competition, and that will continue to be true through the rest of our lives. Indeed, we will move up from 70 percent to probably even more—80, 90 percent.

Because of the baby boom, 85 percent of those who will be in the work force in the year 2001 are already adults, and most are already at work. We face a reality for the next two decades that we are going to make it or break it with the people who are already at work. That has very real implications for education. The people who are going to be changing occupations three times and jobs six to seven times are the only workers we are going to have. To face this great change, they must be retrained, reeducated, retooled. Who's going to do that? That is the challenge for education and business.

What will flexibility require?

Yet for all of these things that we know, most of the future is unknown and unknowable. So it's imperative for us to improve our flexibility, our capacity to adapt to the future, however that future may unfold. That's encouraging but also scary. What will it require?

First, business is going to have to take a longer-term view. A major problem today is that American business takes a short-term view. Our competitors, primarily in Japan and Korea, are taking a long-term view. American firms have an obsession with quarterly profits and quarterly earnings. On the other hand, competitors in Japan are concerned about market share. They are thinking long term. If they capture the market, if they dominate the economic scene, then in later times they'll make the money. They'll be able to squeeze out the profits.

Why do we in the United States do such great harm to ourselves for the sake of short-term profits and earnings? Many blame the business schools for this myopia. But to blame the business schools for the short-term focus of business is akin to blaming West Point for the U.S. involvement in wars. The business schools are simply teaching the managers what the market and the environment require. The driving force for this short-term focus is the way the capital markets are operating. When one takes a look at the New York Stock Exchange records, one quickly finds that for the 200 largest corporations, 50-60 percent of their stock is held by pension funds and financial institutions and trust funds. In other words, the major corporations are not owned by individuals: control is in the hands of institutions.

We also see that the behavior of those institutions is oriented toward speculation. In the New York Stock Exchange records you can see that pension funds and institutions in the 1950s accounted for about 25 percent of the value and volume of trade. As their ownership has increased, those institutions last year accounted for 90 percent of the value and volume of trade on the New York Stock Exchange. More important, when you take a look at the individual institutions, you'll find that on average the pensions funds and financial institutions are turning over their entire portfolios in twenty-eight months. Consequently, the total value of the New York Stock Exchange now turns over every two years.

In the mid 1970s that happened every six years. So suddenly, you've got unrelenting pressure from the financial managers' own corporations to get that quick hit, to get those quarterly earnings or they'll sell that stock—a hundred thousand, two hundred thousand, a million shares—just like that.

There are other surveys that go even further. The New York Stock Exchange surveyed 300 of its institutional managers to find out what they looked for in a stock. They found that only 5 percent of those managers looked at the quality of the product of the American firm, at their investment in capital facilities, research and development, at the quality of their management. They looked only at the short-term numbers—the quick hit.

More dramatically, not only are these institutions altering the performance of American corporations, they're incompetent speculators. In 1984, in a roaring stock market, 74 percent of those institutions didn't even hit the Standard & Poor 500 stock index. You'd expect them, with such volume, to hit the average, or maybe do 55 or 60 percent. Three-quarters of them couldn't even hit the average. So they are not only distorting corporate behavior, they're squandering people's pensions. That's one driving force of short-term focus. It's pervasive—and dangerous.

Obstacles in government

A second major set of obstacles we face in adapting and becoming flexible is found within government. Many of you are in government and understand the problems we face in government. One is that we've had two presidents who have run against government, who have attempted by their actions to denigrate it to set a basis for policies against it. And in the process they have created an environment that makes it difficult to help good people in government. Take a look at the Senior Executive Service (SES), for example.

The so-called reforms made in the Social Security system in the late 1970s set the basis for politicization of the Civil Service, particularly at the top levels. Consequently, the General Accounting Office reports that of the 7,000 top people in the SES—those who really play a predominant role in helping run the government, who are the equivalent of the British Civil Service and the French Civil Service, that stand as that underpinning, that backdrop, to counterbalance the fact that political appointees last an average of eighteen months in the government—as the government became less attractive, over half of the SES members resigned, retired, or left it between 1979 and January of 1983. Considerable expertise and experience have been lost, and in the long term, this can do a lot of harm to our government programs and policies.

Equally important, because so many of our programs have been put in place over fifty years incrementally, with little consideration for what exists or the consequences of those programs, the processes of decision making and the influence of government have become fragmented and splintered. For example, to make changes in trade policies requires decisions by as many as twenty-five Executive Branch agencies and nineteen committees and subcommittees of Congress. Thirty-four Executive Branch agencies outside the Office of the

President have some part of the economic policy decision-making responsibilities of the federal government.

One hundred nineteen agencies have some responsibility for pension policies in this country. To undertake actions with very old, very traditional programs—water and power dams, for example—will require decisions from twenty-five congressional subcommittees. And it goes on and on. Power is diffused, and turf battles persist.

I worked for almost a year with the Office of Management and Budget (OMB) during the Carter Administration on details of the reorganization of economic and community development functions. One of the conclusions I reached after that year, was that the possibility of dealing with those changes through massive reorganization of government is nil. It is difficult, if not impossible, for a simple reason. Congress itself must surrender much of the power of subcommittees. That is unlikely to happen. The iron triangle among the agencies, special interests, and Congress is so strong that it is not likely to be broken. The challenge we really face, then, is to find policy mechanisms that can prevent fragmentation and help to focus our efforts. Fortunately, we have some good examples.

The best is the National Security Administration. In the late 1940s we became concerned that our security was threatened by the Soviet Union and that we needed coherence among the departments of Defense, State, the Central Intelligence Agency, and the National Security Agency. We created a neutral broker in the White House, and the National Security Advisor was given a small staff. Their responsibilities were to reconcile and harmonize our defense policies. I think we have come to that point on our economic competitiveness policies. We need to move economic competitivenes to the forefront, recognize the central role it plays in our future, and focus our activities. Again, unless we do that, we are sure to continue to have the present problem wherein unintended consequences become a major byproduct of many of our decisions.

And then, finally, there is the question of workers. Adam Smith said it first and best: "People are the first, the premier resource, and the first responsibility of any nation." And they are. The challenge that we face is how to make full use of our human capital to maintain our competitive edge. We must recognize that although human capital can be our most productive resource, it's the least flexible resource we have. Firms can simply abandon a plant, buy new technology off the shelf, or create it. But to change human capital is difficult because it involves dealing with voters, with attitudes, and with the process of learning. It's difficult to make that transition.

A national training and adjustment strategy

As a country, we're only partially set up to make the necessary adaptations and to help our workers make them. We need to look carefully at devising some form of cooperative federal government/state government/local government/business/union/employer strategy national training and adjustment strategy to help us make those adaptations.

I see that process as consisting of several parts. One of the basic elements is to consider maintaining the investments that are going to be required to ensure that our educational institutions have state-of-the-art facilities and equipment. One of the studies by the Business-Higher Education Forum, repeatedly brought to our attention, as did the National Science Foundation, that our educational facilities, the infrastructure, our equipment, are rapidly becoming obsolete. We need to find the ways and the money to make sure that we have state-of-the-art equipment and facilities and teaching skills.

Then we will need to make sure that our labor market adjustment mechanism works—the employment security system, that facility that helps employers find workers and workers find jobs. It doesn't work today! In fact, it has become a somnolent system by and large. Today, what we find is that only sixteen of the states have computerized their operations. We also find that fewer than 7 percent of employers even list their jobs with the state employment service. And we further find that most of the jobs now placed through the state employment service are very menial, nonskilled jobs. Workers are losing a major source of testing and counseling, a way to find out what they require to meet the job demands of employers. And employers are missing a major source of workers. It's largely because we've been unimaginative and have not put up money for the challenge. We have collected a billion dollars to operate that system, but it's being held in the trust funds to finance the national debt, to meet other challenges.

We require a comprehensive displaced worker program. Two million people a year are now being displaced from their jobs because of technological and trade changes. The country is not set up with a financing system that allows workers to come to educational institutions to make the adjustments. Business, for example, has a rigid set of policies for its training activities. Most of our people are already at work, and a good place for them to get financing for training and training itself is through the business community. And yet when we look at the factors of productivity, capital, technology, and improved workforce performance, we find that our public policy only provides incentive for investment in two of them. Indeed, in the area of tuition tax credits, for every one dollar incentive the private sector is given to invest in training, it is given $3,200 to invest in better machines and technology. That's a problem.

Then there is a whole series of issues that go beyond education and training activities. There's the question of safe, nurturing child care. Today, mothers of half of the children one year of age and under are at work. Most of these women need to and will stay at work. They and their families require good child care. Only 1,800 of our six million employers provide such assistance in any form such as employee benefits, on-site care, or financing. That's another problem.

The final major challenge we face is our aging society. Because we are going to be moving from place to place, we are increasingly going to be concerned about our pensions, since most people's pensions lack portability. Half the employers in this country do not even offer a pension plan. And of those that do, 90 percent require that the worker be employed for ten years or more, so that only half their workers are actually vested in a pension plan. So we have the odd situation of an aging work force with only one out of four workers vested in a pension program. Increasingly, workers are going to become much less reluctant to make the necessary shifts and adaptations. The time has come for us to find ways to tie pensions to the workers and not to the jobs. Then people can move from occupation to occupation, job to job, industry to industry, place to place, knowing they will have a secure, well-financed retirement.

In sum, the forte of our economic system has been our ability to change with change—our flexibility, our capacity to adapt. That has underpinned our enthusiasm for change; it has underpinned the dynamic economy we have that is now threatened by the pervasive inflexibility that permeates our society. The old nineteenth-century stockbroker contemporary of Jay Gould and Jim Fisk, Uncle Daniel Drew, said that all he ever wanted out of deal was a little unfair advantage. In effect, our flexibility has been our unfair advantage. How well and how quickly we can recapture that in education, business, government, and society in general, will in large measure determine our economic future.

3

Developing Inner-City Business

James Howell

The author is senior vice president and chief economist for the Bank of Boston. He has also served as economic advisor to the Assistant Secretary of Commerce for Economic Affairs.

There are 275 urban areas in the United States; two-thirds of the U.S. population lives in these areas. This includes between 35 and 40 million Americans trapped in what have become virtual "foreign enclaves" because they are separated from the mainstream of urban life. These are disaffected individuals who have no confidence in working within the system of the market economy and reaching upward to economic opportunity. Crowded into these same areas are many urban colleges and universities facing an increasingly hostile environment. Such an environment demands that we contribute more to the dynamic affairs of the communities in which we are residents.

The need: economic enfranchisement

What is needed is the economic enfranchisement—through small-business development—of minorities and other individuals in these enclaves. Small or minority business development programs have been tried many times but generally do not work because of logjams on bureaucratic details and processes or the failure to understand properly each participant's role.

Let me give you an example. Consider the issue of capital access. When small business persons come into a bank from the inner city, they are often so poorly prepared that we immediately turn them down and send them back out on the street. We do that because we are in the business of lending money for which we are to be repaid. As a result, the banker will usually develop a less receptive attitude toward new inner-city lending because of the poor preparation of the small business person. And, at the same time, the individual we turned down understandably comes to view bankers in less than favorable terms. As a result, we and the community lose.

Now let's look at the same issue from another perspective. City economic development officials also look at the situation differently than do bankers. Their view is, Why don't the bankers create a $25-million loan pool through which the economic development officials can ladle out loans and money as they see fit? But again, to the banker, matters are not so simple: business loans must not only be repaid, but each request for credit can only be judged on a deal-by-deal basis.

The net result of these differing viewpoints is that matters get stuck and nothing happens.

Let me now address the solution for this problem. In Boston, for the past several years we have been working through a nonprofit organization known as the Council for Economic Action to put together the elements of a small business development program in partnership with other banks and a large urban university—Boston University. The participating banks have combined assets of roughly $150 billion. Our agenda was to design a program that had three key elements of small business success: market, management, and capital.

The key elements

During my childhood years in Texas, my mother used to tell me that I would never amount to a hill of beans (although the exact value of a hill of beans still remains a mystery to me). She simply said that fortune rewards the prepared mind. We have taken that very theme for our small-business development program and restructured it as follows: economic opportunity rewards the prepared individual. As our work evolved, we divided the program into its key elements.

Market identification. The Council for Economic Action developed a systematic program to examine an urban area for industries having fewer than the expected number of firms. These areas are prime targets for new entrant activity. If an industry has fewer than the expected number of firms, then new entrants will be accelerated and thus will be prime targets for our new business start-ups because they have a higher probability of success.

Management training. The Boston University School of Management designed two education modules—a short course of twelve hours and a longer course of forty-eight hours. The short course usually meets on two Saturdays, six hours each, and costs participants $60.00. We believe, up front, that the way you handle successful small business development is to avoid subsidizing it. New entrepreneurial discipline can be identified through these small financial hurdles, and this provides a successful means of winnowing out the serious from the unserious. The long course is $600.00 and is spread over four months. When individuals come out of that course, they have a business plan in their hands and are well prepared to meet the banker.

Access to capital. Through the Council for Economic Action, we coordinated the small business person's first meeting with the bank lending officers. So when our students come out of the Boston University program, they have a fundamental grounding about their industry and its market and have a business plan. They may not have gone to the Harvard Business School, but our students are going to be well prepared, and we are asking the banks to consider them on a deal-by-deal basis at market-rate lending. As we ask the banks to consider making these loans, we will enhance the *quality* as well as the *volume* of the deal flow—both factors that are vitally important to successful bank lending.

The vital role of outreach

Once the above elements are in place, we still have to consider outreach, for we found out that even if we know in which industries new entrants or firms are likely to succeed, even if we have a business training program and open the door at Boston University, real-world experience has taught that nobody will show up. A solid outreach program must play a role. Consequently, we designed and implemented a student outreach program in the inner city of Boston, through the black churches, through the black and Hispanic radio stations, and through the neighborhood media.

The day before we launched the program, a colleague in my bank told me that he doubted whether anyone would show up after we ran the outreach program. But within two weeks after the first cycle of the outreach program in the inner city was completed, we had a thousand legitimate inquiries from individuals who asked for a chance to go to the short course. It turned out that 180 persons completed the short course in the first four cycles, and then forty went on to the long course.

Council staff assisted them with technical assistance on an "as needed" basis. This fall, there will be additioanl course offerings as well as new and exciting options. For example, Boston University will experiment with a Kenmore Square "walk-in" technical assistance office in a branch of the Bank of Boston. The office will be staffed by MBA students and will be open two evenings a week.

The results

The results in Boston are impressive: in the first eighteen months, twenty-six new businesses have been started—80 percent minority, 70 percent female, $747,000 worth of capital financing, of which $426,000 came from banks—and sixty-five permanent jobs have been created. We are now in the process of recycling or restarting the educational process in the summer and into the fall, and then again each spring, at which time new businesses will be formed. It is the replication of that process, year in and year out, that makes the difference. Over the first three years, we will generate seventy-five new businesses in Boston's inner city—all owned by individuals who previously wondered whether they could make it in the dynamic affairs of our economy.

We are also encouraging existing firms in undersupplied industries to expand. We think we can raise the targeted number of firms that are strengthened and expanded to several hundred per year. We are also examining the possibility of targeting firms that have succession problems, most of which are minority firms. The problem is simply stated: the heirs to established businesses in the inner city generally have little or no interest in carrying on the family business. These heirs, again, constitute excellent prospects for new minority business ownership.

Where is the Boston model headed? Why has it worked, and what is its future? The Boston model has already spread to Stockton, California, and to Milwaukee. Through a U.S. Department of Housing and Urban Development (HUD) grant, we are in Chattanooga, Norfolk, Portsmouth, and Lake County, with the likelihood of expanding to several new sites around the country. The key to all this is finding the components in a community that are needed to make the program work: banks willing to take part in the program; individuals who are disaffected; and an academic institution that wants to play an innovative role in its community.

Why has this program worked so well? We have stayed with it, we have been realistic, and we have concentrated on thinking small. Programs succeed, in my opinion, because they are kept well within manageable dimensions.

We have set goals. The goals in Chattanooga, for example, will be to create thirty-five to forty new businesses in twenty-four months and to expand and diversify 100 businesses in undersupplied industries in the same period. Experience teaches that if you set goals, you will come closer to achieving them.

More than anything else, I think the program has worked because it has benefited from others that have not worked. The essence of the program's success does not lie in any new and unique ideas, but rather in the way the elements for success are brought together. And, in the final analysis, it is the *audacity* to succeed that has made the difference.

4

Transferring Technologies to Industry

David H. Swanson

The author is director of the Center for Industrial Research and Service of Iowa State University and chairman of the Iowa High Technology Council. He was formerly director of the Iowa Development Commission.

Public policies in the 1980s have increasingly concentrated on the need for economic growth. As the decade has progressed, discussions of economic development have focused chiefly on the development of growth industries in the private sector. This examination has revealed that small businesses, particularly in the service sectors, have created the most jobs. There has also been increasing national awareness of the role of technology, especially advanced technologies, in increasing the new products, processes, and systems needed to improve the nation's competitive edge in international trade. States have perceived that advanced-technology industries and developed local businesses are the answer to their need for employment opportunities, revenues, and political continuity. The approach to creating economic growth has shifted dramatically from attracting mature industries to developing advance-technology industries. Accompanying this trend is the growing awareness that modernizing existing industries and businesses is an integral part of economic development.

This dramatic shift in focus from large, relatively mature industries to smaller, advanced-technology businesses places greater pressures on higher education to become an active, rather than passive, partner in economic development.

New processes and products are now recognized as vital components of economic development. Higher education institutions are increasingly seen as creators of those products and processes. The research and ideas generated by scientists and experts at a university are considered vital to economic development. Political, economic, and peer pressures compel higher education institutions to develop ideas, produce basic and applied research, educate people to work in an advanced technological society, and share knowledge with the public and industry.

Technology transfer

The current public interest in technology transfer stems largely from concern about employment opportunities. Other concerns include modernizing industry, international competition, and the advancement of society's knowledge base, but quite clearly, the public wants employment opportunities and industry wants competitive advantages. As the costs of business increase, international competition intensifies, and products become more complex and interrelated, different sectors of society need to share research costs and find the products and processes that will enable industry to thrive. The need to find a strong competitive advantage is now apparent in industry, business, government, community, and education—and, increasingly, funds are shifted to areas of potential competitive advantage.

The development of concepts, materials, systems, equipment, instruments, knowledge, and other products of the creative processes are goals higher education shares with industry. These aims are not always identical or similar in time frame or environment, but more and more, various groups look to higher education to help generate economic benefits for localities, firms, state, and national systems. Difficulties frequently arise in determining how to share that information with those outside the university and college and how to transmit needs to researchers. Classroom teaching is an excellent and proven vehicle for technology transfer, but it cannot accommodate all audiences and avenues of communication.

The flow of ideas from their source and the implementation of technology transfer require not only the generation of an idea but also its evaluation, production, and application. Most studies indicate that the process of moving an idea from the laboratory to common public usage takes an average of 15-20 years. The computer, for example, is now over forty years old. The complex process of transferring research results into a widely accepted commercial product has not been well understood. Diffusion theories, concepts of adoption processes, and education theories have provided usable insights, but much has yet to be learned about how the technology transfer process works and how to accelerate it.

The role of the university in transferring technologies has been the focus of several studies, all of which demonstrate that higher education institutions have a definite role to play. Recent studies on manufacturing and other business needs may provide insight into those roles and their complexities. Manufacturers believe higher education has a strong role in developing and transferring technology but is not the only participant. The university is therefore a partner in this service but not the sole provider. Its role in economic growth consists of development, coordination, communication, needs assessment, integration, and cooperation.

study of industries' needs in Iowa

The perspective of industry is critical to determining higher education's role in technology. That is why the Center for Industrial Research and Service (CIRAS) conducted a survey in 1984 of the research needs of industries in the State of Iowa. There is no doubt that technology will have considerable impact on manufacturers and processors; less than 3 percent of manfacturers surveyed in 1984 felt technology would have no effect on their business during the next

Table 1
Survey on Impact of Technology in Five Years

| | Percent Response | | | |
Impact	Process	Product	Material	Information Needs
Great	13.4	12.5	8.3	14.9
Considerable	31.9	27.1	23.0	32.6
Some	38.9	40.0	45.5	37.9
Little	14.1	17.8	20.6	11.7
None	1.4	2.1	3.3	2.8

Source: Center for Industrial Research and Service (CIRAS) Survey of Research Needs of Iowa Industry, 1984.

five years. Significant impact was anticipated on products, processes, materials, and the information needed to operate. Forty-seven percent of the firms perceived a greater need for technical information in the next five years and 45 percent foresaw major technological changes in their manufacturing processes. (See Table 1.)

Manfacturers did not anticipate these needs because of any negative view of their firms. Thirty-three percent of the executives felt their processes were already advanced or very advanced, 43 percent felt their products were advanced, 34 percent their materials, and 27 percent their research. The only area wherein executive questioned their capabilities was research, for which they considered their level of technology low (29 percent). The low level undoubtedly results from smaller firms difficulty in maintaining any research capability. (See Table 2.)

Table 2
Level of Technology in Firm

Level	Percent Response			
	Process	Product	Material	Research
Very Advanced	4.6	8.6	4.6	7.4
Advanced	29.1	34.5	29.4	20.3
Medium	53.4	45.6	53.0	42.6
Low	12.6	11.0	12.3	29.3

Source: CIRAS Survey of Research Needs of Iowa Industy, 1984.

Obtaining information

Manufacturing exectives (Iowa) have few doubts about how they currently obtain technical information or where they prefer to obtain it: largely through the market process and through their own personal efforts. Manufacturing representatives, sales representatives, suppliers, trade associations, personal reading and research, and conferences are the current sources consulted on new technologies. But manufacturers also desire to consult colleges and universities. (See Table 3.)

The manufacturers consult a variety of sources for information on technology and research, including universities, consultants, laboratories, and government. But the sources they currently use are not necessarily those they would prefer. Universities, colleges, and government laboratories are also desired sources. Available data suggest that universities and colleges, especially if they collaborated with equipment manufactures and associations, could become more effective forces in the transfer of technology. (See Table 4.)

Manufacturers are especially interested in information on products new to the market place, processes, equipment, and materials. They have less interest in the latest information on science and technology. (See Table 5.)

Table 3
Current Sources of Information

		Percent Response	
Rank	Source	Used	Not Used
1	Manufacturing Representatives	55	45
2	Sales Representatives	54	46
3	Trade Associations	52	48
4	Magazines	49	51
5	Personal Efforts	47	53
6	Suppliers	42	58
7	Conferences	41	59
8	Universities & Colleges	31	69
9	Journals	28	72
10	Company Research Dept. in Iowa	22	78
11	Company Research Dept. not in Iowa	15	85
12	Private Laboratories	14	86
13	Friends	12	88
14	Government Laboratories	7	93
15	Television	3	97

Source: CIRAS Survey of Research Needs of Iowa Industry, 1984.

Table 4
Desired Sources of Information/Research: Outside the Firm

		Percent Response	
Rank	Source	Will Use	Not Use
1	Equipment Manufacturers	72.4	27.6
2	Trade Associations	69.8	30.2
3	Sales Representatives	58.4	41.6
4	Universities and Colleges	57.1	42.9
5	Magazines	49.9	52.1
6	Consultants	34.8	65.2
7	Private Laboratories	33.5	66.5
8	Government Laboratories	20.6	79.4
9	Government	12.7	87.3
10	Chamber of Commerce	11.4	88.6
11	Others	6.7	93.3

Source: CIRAS Survey of Research Needs of Iowa Industry, 1984.

Table 5
Information Needs

Rank	Source	Percent Response	
		Yes	*No*
1	New Products	63	37
2	Processing Equipment	61	39
3	Materials	56	44
4	Existing Products	47	53
5	Market Potential	47	53
6	Science	11	89
7	General Information	10	90

Source: CIRAS Survey of Research Needs of Iowa Industry, 1984.

Industries have also emphasized the need for cooperative industry/university research projects and encouraging company investment in its own research. The development of university research capabilities and intercompany relationships is considered a viable option worth pursuing. Most of the responding manufacturers favored research facilities near research universities, although only 36 percent anticipated an immediate benefit to their firm. (See Table 6.)

Table 6
Preferences on Aiding Industrial Research

Rank		Percent Response	
		Yes	*Not Ranked*
1	Engaging in joint industry/university research	47	53
2	Encourage company investment in research	45	55
3	Provide tax incentives for private research	44	56
4	Establish facilities at universities for industrial research	37	63
5	Expand universities research capability	36	64
6	Collaborate on intercompany research	35	65
7	Expand federal laboratories	14	86

Source: CIRAS Survey of Research Needs of Iowa Industry, 1984.

Among the firms anticipating benefits, most felt that access to university expertise and facilities and the possiblity of reducing their research costs were the most attractive features of a research facility. Executives also believed that university/industry research should be related to application—not basic sciences. They also favored research parks with permanent facilities, although a large number of firms did express a preference for a facility permitting temporary occupancy.

Company size

Company size was a key factor in the responses on current level of technology. Eighty-one percent of the largest firms considered their production processes advanced, compared with only 38 percent of the smallest firms. A similar pattern, although not as pronounced, arose in other areas.

Surprisingly, the size of the firm had virtually no influence on the preferred source or current source of technical information. Notable exceptions were the large companies, which preferred universities and colleges as a source in addition to consultants and private and government laboratories.

The current sources used in obtaining technical information varied in only a few areas. The smaller firms rely on the personal efforts of their chief executives. Large firms use consultants, universities, and laboratories, as well as their own research staffs.

Higher education's role

Industry desires higher education's informational and technical expertise more than that of government entities. Education as a source of technical information is not currently being utilized to its fullest extent. Several surveys support these statements. A 1982 survey indicated that industry expected higher education institutions to develop, and to aid in the development of, technologies; and 63 percent expected them to help transfer technology. (See Tables 7 and 8.)

The question generally arises as to how to transfer information effectively to industry. Industry has offered a consistent response. Executives want information in short bulletins written in a management or engineering writing style. They also favor conferences and workshops rather than television or faculty exchanges. Based on the sophistication of the industries and size, a one-page summary and possible follow-up report and development workshop are the best methods for reaching the manufacturing executive. (See Tables 9 and 10.)

The university/college role in transferring technology necessitates an understanding of the need for two-way communication with industry about the coordination of roles of current technology suppliers and about certain marketing principle. Although higher education is an excellent information developer, integrator, assimilator, and communicator, it has certain shortcomings. It does not generate or store information, nor is it particularly responsive and attuned to the needs of industry. Like government laboratories, it directs research toward a specific need—and shares with secondary markets only after that primary need has been satisfied. Therefore, any major improvements in the transfer of technology will require some early integration of the needs and participation of industry with university programs.

Current information systems are remarkably successful in reaching their primary targets. Researchers seeking to satisfy their own curiosities, impress peers, advance knowledge, satisfy a contractor, or publish generally accomplish

Table 7
Expectations to Develop New Technology (percents of survey responses)

	Equipment Manufacturers	My Company	Universities & Colleges	Trade Associations	Magazines & Journals	Government Labs	Consultants
Checked this source	83*	65	61	60	50	49	46
Ranked							
1	44*	19*	6	7	2	1	1
2	14	11	15*	17*	7	4	4
3	7	10	12	14	8	6	6
4	4	6	10	9	9*	7	7
5	2	5	7	5	5	7	11*
6	1	5	6	4	9	6	10
7	1	3	2	1	9	16*	6
Not selected	17	35	39	40	50	51	54

*Highest frequency

Table 8
Expectations to Transfer Technology (percents of survey responses)

	Trade Associations	Equipment Manufacturers	Magazines & Journals	Universities & Colleges	My Company	Consultants	Government Labs
Checked this source	78*	74	73	63	54	49	48
Ranked							
1	18	28*	12	8	12*	1	1
2	22*	15	14	9	7	4	3
3	14	11	16*	11	7	4	3
4	9	7	11	12*	4	7	5
5	3	4	6	9	6	10	9
6	1	2	3	6	7	12*	8
7	1	1	2	2	6	9	16*
Not selected	22	26	27	37	46	51	52

*Highest frequency

Table 9
Language Style

		Percent Response	
Rank	Style	Yes	No
1	Management	50	50
2	Engineering	40	60
3	General Writing	37	63
4	Sales Literature	37	63
5	Scientific	19	81

Source: CIRAS Survey of Research Needs of Iowa Industry, 1984.

Table 10
Ways to Accelerate Technology Transfer

		Percent Response	
Rank	Method	Yes	No
1	Bulletins	81	19
2	Conference and Workshops	61	39
3	Individual Technical Support	37	63
4	Classes and Seminars	37	63
5	Conferences with Other Companies	30	70
6	Computer Access to Dat	27	73
7	Faculty/Industry Exchange	22	78
8	Film	12	88
9	Telvision	10	90
10	Other	3	97

Source: CIRAS Survey of Research Needs of Iowa Industry, 1984.

those goals. Papers are prepared, journal articles written, and knowledge presented to a government agency. It is when this information is expanded to groups for which it was not orginally intended that the difficulties of technology transfer occur: secondary markets are always more difficult to penetrate. Technology must be restructured or restated to match the needs of secondary markets. Thus, the major acceleration in the transfer of technology requires the university or college to identify technical and economic needs of private enterprise. To do so, institutions may need to shift the focus of their research and open up communications with industry.

Surveys of manufacturers, developing university/industry research relationships, increased public-sector investment in applied research, and increasing political interest in economic development have heightened education's role in developing and transferring technology to industry. Education is perceived as a depository and developer of technology that is critical to economic development. Education has the capabilities to communicate complex science, research, and technology to the public. It also has the capability to assist in developing new products and processess increasingly demanded by the public.

Higher education has an excellent opportunity to contribute significantly to the economic development of national, state, and local economies, not only through its attraction and training of students but through an expanding role in the transfer of technology. The full development of these potentials will require study, understanding, awareness, cooperation, coordination, and commitment. Clearly another window of opportunity has opened for colleges and universities.

5

State Initiatives in Economic Development: Four Successful Strategies

Charles Bartsch

The author is a senior policy analyst specializing in economic development and education issues at the Northeast-Midwest Institute and director of its Economic Development and Human Resources group.

For the economic development practitioner, greater university participation in small business development and other economic development activities has been a welcome if not fully understood phenomenon that has brought new resources into the economic development inventory.

The Northeast-Midwest Institute is an advocacy and research organization that looks at issues of interest and concern to the eighteen states in our Northeast-Midwest region.

As the economies of the Northeast and Midwest have improved, we have been able to use educational resources to promote economic development because educational resources in those states have not diminished even in times of financial shortfalls.

Tapping state and local resources

Economic development depends on the availability of venture capital and other financial resources, human resources, infrastructure and space to hatch new enterprises, and also entrepreneurs. As states are taking increasing responsibility for meeting each of these needs, universities are becoming larger players in state and local development strategies—and they should. Local governments are beginning to realize that universities have considerable and diverse resources that they can tap to the mutual benefit of both local governments and universities. And these resources take on growing importance in a time of federal budget cuts and fiscal restraints. For many universities, this unaccustomed role brings new challenges and new opportunities. Although no two schools and no two states are doing exactly the same thing, there are a lot of successes out there, and a lot of successes waiting to happen, too.

These successes are based on frank dialogue among state and local government officials, university officials, private business owners, and managers. The discussions link the academic and research strengths of universities with the economic labor force and quality-of-life advantages of the university communities.

I'd like to focus on four types of state sponsored collaboration: developing new technologies and new products; advancing technologies and processes for existing industries; assisting the development of new small businesses; and related to this, providing business growth in incubators—the environment necessary for business to flourish.

Developing new technologies and products

Universities' achievements in research have traditionally been recognized, but promoting the commercial applicability of research and taking the steps from research results to market are new directions that institutions are beginning to take. State development agencies are increasingly urging that government, business, and university join forces to exploit the commercial and business opportunities of applied research. These collaborations can pay handsome dividends in terms of economic development, business generated, jobs created, and tax revenues paid to local government. These collaborations can also provide opportunities for faculty members and students and often bring revenues and royalties to their sponsoring institutions.

Two types of strategies are pursued: attracting existing high-tech industries and developing new firms to improve technology transfer systems. Last year in Texas, public and private sector officials joined and committed staff abilities and money to the University of Texas. In conjunction with the university, they convinced the Microelectronic and Computer Consortium, a group of about fifteen high-tech companies devoted to research and development, to locate in Austin. The consortium chairman said that Austin was chosen because of the state's commitment to make the University of Texas a world-class leader in computer sciences and electrical engineering.

Michigan leaders recognized that successfully incorporating new technology into an economic development strategy called for public-sector intervention at two stages: first, initial support of research, and then, promotion of the commercial application of research results. Accordingly, the Michigan Biotechnology Institute (MBI) was launched in conjunction with Michigan State University (MSU) to promote increased commercial applications of biotech discoveries. One of the things MBI did was to develop a technology resource center. It also authorized six joint MBI/MSU professorships and directed a number of the resource research results toward the forestry and food-processing industries, which the Michigan Economic Development Office has targeted for Michigan's economic revitalization and diversification.

The nation's most widely known program is Pennsylvania's Ben Franklin Partnership. This partnership is not only one of the earliest programs, but it is also one of the most successful. It created thousands of jobs and generated a lot of tax revenue.

Developing new technologies for existing industries

In the Northeast and Midwest, we don't like to use the words "Rust Belt." "Industrial Heartland" is more our term. A number of initiatives here have been based on bringing new technology to existing industry. In fact, university expertise and university contributions have provided substance and depth in several state sponsored economic development initiatives. The Thomas Alva Edison Program has concentrated heavily on existing industries. It is premised on the idea that Ohioans can make do with what can work and prosper with what they've got. Building on its base is a very important premise. A lot of states have spent and wasted a lot of money pursuing the elusive high-tech dream, when in fact high technology can be successfully applied to existing industries, as it has been in Ohio and Michigan.

The Thomas Alva Edison Program has several technolgy centers. Two are for advanced manufacturing—at the University of Cincinnati and at Cleveland State University. Polymer research is underway at Case Western University. Welding research is undertaken at Ohio State University in Columbus. All of the work is done in conjunction with corporate sponsors. Schools do general applied, as well as proprietary, research. The Ben Franklin Partnership is accomplishing some very interesting things in this area. Lehigh University is promoting computer applications in the glass industry and Ohio State is working on microcomputer technology and design for casting and foundries.

A good example is Michigan's Industrial Technology Institute (ITI), at the University of Michigan, which specializes in the development of automated manufacturing and robotics. Its goal is to create the factory of the future, and it has started to do that. ITI hopes to make manufacturing more adaptable to fluctuations in market demand, materials, and retooling, to make manufacturing more competitive. The State of Michigan provided $17.5 million to ITI in 1982, at a time when the state was facing severe financial problems. This was a significant commitment that sent a clear signal to business leaders in the state, and foundations in the state have come up with a lot more money to support this commitment.

Small business development

Small businesses are and probably will continue to be the country's major employer. They are the major source of new jobs. Universities have a key role to play in nurturing small business development. Let me just cite a few examples: in 1982 Ohio State University created the Innovation Center and Research Park to promote economic growth in southeastern Ohio. This is a very depressed area with few economic bases. The purpose was to encourage the faculty to go out and help develop entrepreneurship and new businesses. Basically, they are in the business of "birthing" new companies. They have had some successes. They are providing—through an incubator facility, cheap rent, and through faculty and graduate students—needed technical assistance. Both resources have been critical to new business development in this area.

The Connecticut Small Business Development Center works with the business school at the University of Connecticut to provide various types of free or low-cost assistance to new and expanding businesses, including marketing, pre-venture feasibility studies, financial planning, record keeping, and business plan development. These services are provided through individual counseling, workshops, and assistance from the faculty. Unlike similar endeavors that focus mostly on emerging companies, the Connecticut Center places considerable emphasis on existing businesses. Helping them expand, helping them modernize, and helping them stay are very important functions. These efforts have yielded good dividends to the state.

Georgia's Advanced Technology Center has worked with engineers who have a lot of enthusiasm, a lot of technical knowledge, and no business skills. The center takes that enthusiasm and knowledge and translates them into business development.

Business incubators

Universities frequently sponsor small business incubators in their efforts to promote new business development. These are often encouraged by state development agencies. Some states offer start-up or operating assistance. Incubators can be an important part of the nurturing necessary for small businesses to grow and thrive. Providing incubators is a logical next step in many university economic development efforts. Although many incubators operate independently of university ties, there are clear advantages to university sponsorship.

The firms are in a much better position to take advantage of technology-related research, to tie into university resource networks, and to benefit from the university's stature in the community. Several large and growing incubators are now in place under university auspices, including Science Park in New Haven, Connecticut, and the University City Science Center in Philadelphia. The Ben Franklin program has sponsored a number of incubators as has the Thomas Alva Edison program, linking them to their technology centers and enjoying some measure of success.

The Northeast-Midwest Institute has published a number of monographs on various economic development and education issues. *Partners and Growth* looked at university and state linkages. Another one is soon to appear, called *The Development Triangle,* on the role of community colleges in economic development. We have also convened a task force of public and private-sector officials, chaired by Pat Choate of TRW, Inc. This task force will soon be reporting its findings.

An International
Perspective

6

Developing International Trade at the Local Level

Andrew Young

The author is mayor of the City of Atlanta, Georgia. He has served as U.S. Ambassador to the United Nations and as a member of the Cabinet and the National Security Council.

This is a subject dear to my heart and one essential to the survival not only of the academic community but of the nation's economy.

In 1978, when I was in Nigeria, I bumped into an American businessman who was in the process of negotiating a contract with the Nigerian government to put together a fertilizer plant. The U.S. company had bid $460 million and a Japanese-Italian consortium had bid $400 million, and it just didn't seem there was any way an American company could get that contract. But I had a meeting set up with the head of Nigeria, who was an engineer and a good friend of mine. In joking around, since the United States was then running about a $27-billion trade deficit with Nigeria, largely because of oil, I poked fun at him a little and said, "You know, if you were making suits I'd say you'd do well with Italians, but Americans know about fertilizer." In the course of jesting back and forth, and my fearing that we had no chance for the contract, he said, "You know, if you could find a way to get the bid down just a little, we really want to give the contract to an American company because they will be operating in English and it will really be a lot easier for our people to learn."

And then suddenly it clicked for me. This was a company based in Houston, and I realized that at that time there were about 5,000 Nigerian students in the Houston area. (We had almost 5,000 Nigerian students in the Atlanta area, too.) I began to ask myself how many students at Rice, at Texas Southern, at all of the universities in the Houston area, might be good engineering students. I said to him, "I think we can probably get this company to come down a bit. But I think what they could do for you, in addition to putting together a good turnkey project, is to recruit Nigerian students who are already in the United States and involve them in a similar kind of plant in the U.S. By the time this plant is completed we will have trained a work force of Nigerian students who are able to run it so it's not just a turnkey project that you will have to pay Japanese and Italians to manage for the next twenty years. It will be a complete project that can be Nigerian almost from the moment it's completed." He said, "If you can do that and get them to come down some $30 million, I think we've got a deal."

The university connection

That university connection was worth $30 million on a $460-million project. It didn't require anything extra from the company. It essentially required only that American business establish an active relationship with its university system. Now, we already have an active relationship with our universities for research and development. We already offer most of the education needed by the business community, but we've never thought of the university, for the most part, as part of the marketing network of the economy of the United States of America. That's essentially what I would like to propose.

The marketing side, it seems to me, is the critical issue. There is marketing potential in our university system we have not yet begun to explore. On the campuses of almost every university, particularly those like Georgia Institute of Technology and Atlanta University, for the past hundred years, and at Georgia State more recently, on any given day there are students from seventy or eighty different countries. And the alumni of these institutions over the last hundred years, located around the world, constitute a worldwide marketing network that's almost never utilized in marketing the goods and services produced in the United States of America.

Learning how to trade

I'm convinced that our economy is in trouble if we don't learn how to trade. We cannot run a government with a $2-trillion budget deficit, an annual budget deficit in the area of $2 billion, and a trade deficit of $150 billion. Every billion dollars we incur in trade deficit costs somewhere between thirty and forty thousand jobs. And when you multiply that out, you can see that unemployment in the U.S. is almost directly correlated to the trade deficit we are experiencing.

I had that idea brought home to me here in Atlanta when another friend of mine visited, who also happened to be Nigerian. There had been a notice in the paper that *Scientific Atlanta* was going to have to lay off 400 people. About that time this friend of mine came to town, and I asked him how the new federal capital was going. He said, "Well, it's going pretty well, but we're having trouble; nobody is going to believe that we are really moving to the new federal capital. We had hoped to televise it, but we find now that we can't get the television operation together. They say it will take anywhere from four to six months to do that." I said, "Have you explored some of the earth station satellite systems?" He said, "No, we haven't." But again, it was a German-Japanese consortium that had said it would take four to six months. I said, "Look, if you've got an extra day I'd like to send you out to talk to our people in Atlanta." So they went out and talked to *Scientific Atlanta* and it turned out, as result of that conversation, that the kind of equipment they needed was already on hand. Since we're also a city that has Lockheed (they make the C-130s and everybody in the world has got a C-130), we arranged to have two Nigerian C-130s flown in for routine servicing, loaded up the *Scientific Atlanta* equipment, sent the technicians, and installed the system in two weeks.

I went over to Nigeria about six months later. My friend was amazed and didn't know how we did it, because the price actually charged was about one-third that quoted by the other consortium. The difference was that these countries build in what I call a "corruption tax." They figure it takes so much foolishness and red tape to get something done, they factor all that into the price, figure they are going to have to pay off everybody to get a job done and it's going to be long and slow. When you find a way to deal at the top level, particularly cutting short the time of a transaction through some kind of personal contact, it's possible to do the job more quickly and cheaply.

Atlanta as an international trade center

I see this city of ours as a potential trading company. I think the twenty-nine colleges and universities in our metropolitan area are basic to the nature of that trading company. Talking to somebody from Iowa State, I got a very good idea. He said that Iowa State University publishes a book of graduates of Iowa State who are working and living overseas and who were foreign students. I bet if we did that for the twenty-nine colleges and universities in the Atlanta area, we would find a contact in just about every nation in the world who knows Atlanta, knows the American business community to some extent, and has pretty good connections in either government or business in their own countries. Anybody who has the advantage of an American education and lives in another part of the world is going to be doing pretty well. We are now in the process of gearing up the city as a trading company because we've got to solve this problem of how America can overcome its trade deficit and do business overseas.

When you come right down to it, that was my basic reason for running for mayor. I felt that it was going to be extremely difficult to make ends meet in any city, knowing the kinds of things that were going to happen, not knowing the strategy would be named Gramm-Rudman but knowing that a country that is $2 trillion in debt could not continue to give money to its cities. More and more, cities were going to have to find ways to generate new income, and the money was going to have to come from the private sector if growth was to occur. And I thought if any city could become a model for international trade and investment, it was Atlanta. We had everything going for us—mainly an airport having a capacity of about 2,239 flights per day, with flights to 200 cities many times a day, and on any given day there have been between 1,950 and 2,000 flights. That in itself made it possible for us to think of ourselves as a city of the future, a city truly of the twenty-first century, a global city that could begin not only to internationalize our own local economy, but to help the economy of the United States of America to become more and more international.

Attracting investment

And we have been approaching that. I must confess that we've done better in attracting investments than in selling abroad. I thought that was going to be the hard part, but over the last three years we have attracted $29.5 billion worth of new investment into this city. And we've generated more than 300,000 new jobs. We've been able to do that, in large measure, for both good and bad reasons.

The good reason is that we offer access to the American market place, and anybody in the world who wants to stay in business has to be able to do business within the U.S. market. And because of our accessibility via air, road, and rail, our city is an ideal place from which to do business. More and more companies from abroad are locating in Atlanta as their place of business within the U.S.

We have also established trade missions—to Saudi Arabia, Kuwait, Nigeria, Algeria, Tunisia, Korea, China, India, as well as France, Sweden, Finland, and Belgium. Georgia maintains offices for state industry and trade in Brussels and in Tokyo. We have been mobilized as a state for more than a decade in selling Atlanta and Georgia throughout the world. I came here almost directly from the United Nations, at a time when things that I have mentioned may have been perceived as scandalous here but were considered prophetic around the world. The image of the city was a place open to a global approach to life—we are a city that is half black and half white, and we welcomed Hispanic and Asian minorities. We are perceived abroad as trying aggressively to become an international city. People began to decide that this was a safe haven where they could place their money and where it would be safe and secure over the next forty or fifty years as more and more of the rest of the world's economy became somewhat shaky.

So we are in the midst of tremendous success in terms of attracting new investment. But while we have 470 of the Fortune 500 companies located here, we're still in our infancy as a trade center. We basically are looking to the universities—Georgia Tech, Georgia State, and Atlanta University. They have all pioneereed in establishing some relationships with small business in an attempt to start up technical innovations that turn out to be more and more relevant to the rest of the world. I see that as tremendous potential for trade. I see this as a place from which we can begin to package and finance deals because the market is there and it comes here. It comes to us; it's not a market that we have to go out and seek.

Maximizing marketing services

One of the best examples of retail business here is the Apparel Mart and Merchandise Mart that do, between the two of them, about $9 billion worth of sales in the course of a year. People bring in some 4,000 clothing labels from all over the world, and buyers come in, and under one roof they can do all of their purchasing three or four times a year. That concept of a trade mart, from which almost anything American can be purchased, seems to me to represent the potential of a city like this. We don't manufacture anything, so we have to figure out ways to stay viable by maximizing our services, and marketing has to to be one of our major assets. It has to be something we cultivate.

The same can be true of almost any consortium involving a city and a university. And if cities begin to see their universities not just as a place for training people for the future but as a potential economic innovator, a potential marketing asset, and make some direct ties—particularly between the foreign student population and the local business community—then they will help America catch up with countries that have essentially been oriented toward trade for their survival for more than 100 years.

Marketing for export

A few years ago Italy was the only industrialized country in the free world that did not run a trade deficit. The reason is that Italy knows it has to sell abroad to survive. Japan and Germany import 80-90 percent of their energy resources. They know they have to import large amounts of raw materials. So over the past decades they have organized their economies around exporting. We never had to export before because we were blessed with a kind of balanced economy. We had raw materials and natural resources here. People wanted our goods and services enough to come and get them. We didn't have to go out and sell. But whenever we have had a product we want to go out and sell, we've been able to do it.

One of the best examples is Coca-Cola, which is also celebrating its 100th anniversary. Coca-Cola is good, but it is a nonessential product: people can live without it. Therefore, it has to be marketed. The taste has to be acquired; one has to begin to believe it's the "real thing." And one can get all caught up in whether it's New Coke or Classic Coke—all of that is just so much foolishness—but see how much money it has made! It has been well marketed. There's no place in the world where one cannot find Coca-Cola. Well, if we can sell Coca-Cola all over the world, why not farm machinery, why not incubators for chickens? Why not solar energy collectors that enable people to cook and to air condition? Why not wind power generators? Why not all the little things we take for granted that the rest of the world needs?

Feeding the hungry through free enterprise

I'm convinced that if we are going to feed the hungry, clothe the naked, and heal the sick, it's going to be done essentially in a free market, in a free enterprise system, and it's going to require the innovation of small business working in conjunction with universities. That's really the strongest weapon we have for our national defense and security. I see this as one of the ways of establishing peace on earth and good will toward men, women, and children.

Our nation relates to other countries in a variety of ways. It's no accident that, while we seem to be at war with Libya, there are Libyans studying in this country and there are American technicians working over there. In countries like Angola or Mozambique, there are missionaries teaching and Gulf Oil is pumping oil. And even though the United States Government does not recognize the government of Angola, when Angola begins to develop its economy and handle its budget and market its oil, it goes to a private company like Arthur D. Little. Angolans are supposed to be communists, according to us, but they depend on the United States for so much, because the Russians are not able to give them the kind of services they need. The Russians handle the fishing off the coast of Angola, but this is what they do: they take 70 percent of the fish back to Russia, give 20 percent of the fish to the Cubans, and the Angolans get the remaining 10 percent.

A capitalist deal is exactly the opposite. The capitalist would get 10 percent and leave 90 percent with the country. Even if the exchange is 70/30, it's a better deal. Almost any American company would offer Angola a better deal on its fisheries than it is presently getting from the Russians.

So my contention is that we don't have to go to war with these people to change their minds and to change their system. A combination of our educational system and our productive capacity is the best asset we have to protect our security and our defense all over the world.

When I was with the United Nations, we were in the midst of negotiations with the so-called Marxist Terrorist Patriotic Front. We found ourselves on the island of Malta in an extremely hostile situation. I turned to David Owen, the foreign minister of Britain, and said, "Look, David, we had better take a break and cool this off because we're not getting anywhere at all." Then, in a coffee break during which we were trying to regroup, one of the big, burly African brothers came over to me and said, "Look, I need to talk to you." And I thought, "Oh Lord, have mercy, here we go." I could just see myself getting raked over the coals, because I was looking at these people as the Marxist Terrorist Patriotic Front. That's all I'd ever heard about them and this was my first formal contact with them. The guy asked, "What really happened to the Oakland Raiders?" I thought he was speaking a foreign language. I said, "You mean the football team?" He said, "Yes." I asked him why he was interested. He said, "Well, I was in the Bay area for nine years." He told me he had done his undergraduate work at San Francisco University and gotten his doctorate at Berkeley. And then I suddenly had a change of attitude and realized that maybe this wasn't a Marxist Terrorist movement. I went back and got out the little briefing book produced by the CIA that I had hitherto ignored. I looked in the back, in the fine print, and found there were thirty American-trained Ph.D.'s in this so-called Marxist Terrorist Patriotic Front. All together there were 6,200 people who had degrees beyond a college level from British and American universities. And yet, we had more or less written them off and deemed them enemies. Furthermore, when I began to get to know them, I found that Abel Muzrowea was a bishop of a Methodist church, Joshua Nkoino was a Presbyterian lay preacher, Dominique Sithole was a minister of the United Church of Christ, and Robert Mugabe was a Roman Catholic school teacher and had been headmaster of a Jesuit school for seventeen years. So, in addition to the so-called Marxist rhetoric there was a solid foundation of the Judeo-Christian tradition that came from our missionaries and from our system of higher education.

If we build on those strengths, it seems to me it is possible to put together a global economy that can make sense. It's possible to have fair trade as well as free trade. It's possible for our productive capacity to be increased to meet the needs of people who are hungry.

Look at the Sudan, which right now is in a big furor: $300 billion of oil reserves and natural gas are under the ground there. And the Sudan is the Valley of the Nile, where enough crops could be grown to feed all the world. And yet in the Sudan, right now, there will be over a million people starving. And there will be many, many more people killed because of a struggle there that has taken a certain geopolitical dimension. It's interesting that the guy we think of down there as a Marxist, whom we don't really know, did his undergraduate work at Grinnell and has got a Ph.D. from Iowa State.

The world can make sense. We can pull people like that together. You can't tell me that a person can spend eight years in an American institution and remain totally committed to communism. We have helped raise the expectations and aspirations of people all over the world, but we've not given them the language or the mechanisms to achieve that level of expectation. The Marxists have not really done anything to feed the hungry, or to clothe the naked, or to generate wealth. They do a fair job in terms of distributing the wealth. But in terms of generating new wealth, they've been a total failure. They may have the *language* of revolution. But if you are talking about revolution in terms of goods and services being distributed to people who need them, those kinds of activities only result from the kind of system of which we're a part. But we've not really articulated this. We've not really organized such activities or marketed them on a global basis.

That is our challenge. We have always been a people who don't do what we *ought* to do to until we really *have* to do it—until our survival depends on it. Now I'm convinced that the survival of our system depends on our universities being able to work together with the marketing apparatus of the private sector, and getting a response from and giving leadership to our governments. It seems to me that that's where we finally get to the goal we all share: peace on earth and good will toward all men, women, and children.

7

Bringing Colorado Products to the World Market

Patty Martillaro

The author directs the Small Business
Assistance Center of the University of
Colorado and the affiliated Statewide
Development Corporation.

The University of Colorado Small Business Assistance Center Agricultural Export Project is the university's main economic development and outreach arm to our rural areas. We are a statewide business consulting agency, providing managment and technical assistance to small business. We believe that the future success of Colorado business depends on broadening one's focus and viewing the world as a market place. Because of the severe conditions in the economy, especially within the agricultural industry, we have added exporting and international marketing and consulting to our services and have established the Agricultural Export Project to work specifically with agri-industries.

This project was funded in September by a grant from the U.S Department of Commerce Economic Development Administration. It was designed to provide export consulting to agricultural and agriculture-related businesses in order to develop markets for our agricultural products and to get Colorado further established in international trade.

A cooperative effort

This project has been unique because of the support and cooperation it has received from the many entities working for economic development within the state. We are working with the Colorado International Trade Office, the Colorado Department of Agriculture, the International Trade Administration, the Department of Local Affairs, Division of Commerce and Development, and many support groups ranging from local chambers of commerce to other colleges and universities throughout the state. We are proud of the fact that we have been able to combine our efforts to reach a common goal: the exporting of Colorado agricultural products. Early on we realized that the keys to the success of the project were not only the cooperative efforts of the many groups mentioned but also the capabilities of the person actually delivering the service—the export consultant.

For this we went to the private sector and hired a woman who had many years of hands-on experience in the market place. She has an extensive background in the agricultural field and has worked with Colorado's Celestial Seasonings Company as its international marketing manager. She immediately brought to the position lists of contacts and buyers in several foreign countries. Within the first three months we began to learn what needed to be done in Colorado to get the state's agricultural products into international markets.

We first found that the need for export assistance is enormous. Second, our small companies, for the most part, know little about exporting or even how to get started in exporting. Their idea of exporting has been selling to another state or to even the next county. Third, we found that although we can export value-added food products, we have major problems with exporting food commodities. Fourth, we found we needed a Food-Science Center for product development.

Taking these needs into consideration, we have done several things.

Filling the export needs

First, we organized and conducted workshops thoroughout Colorado to teach basic exporting. These were "how-to" sessions dealing with such topics as letters of credit, taking risks, packaging, labeling—just the basics, from the very beginning. Second, we presented our findings on the need for a Food-Science Center in Colorado to the governor's office. We received the go-ahead to begin putting together a model. We are presently working with Colorado State University, with the Colorado Department of Agriculture, with the Colorado Department of Local Affairs, and with private corporations; key to this activity has been the private corporations' enthusiasm for putting something together.

A task force of representatives of this group and the center has been formed and is undertaking its first project: the cataloguing of what is available in the Colorado State University that can be utilized in the Food-Science Center. This had never been done; no one at the university knew what was actually available and who was doing what. Consequently, we had to take another three steps back and begin by cataloguing that information so that we could determine how to proceed.

The center will be a tremendous asset to the food industry in Colorado when it is fully developed. The Colorado Department of Agriculture has solicited proposals from the rural areas to do feasibility studies for processing plants to be located in their counties. We recently funded two of those projects. The governor's office has set up a hotline to help farmers, ranchers, and agricultural producers locate services and resources and to answer questions about difficulties they encounter.

The Colorado Department of Agriculture has published a newsletter that reaches most of the agricultural industry, to keep members abreast of what is happening in their respective fields and to provide them with information on the agricultural business. We at the center provide articles for this publication.

Our consultant is presently working with forty-five clients, has conducted nine workshops, has represented companies at the International Food Trade Show in California, and the International Pavilion of the National West Stock Show, and has made marketing trips to Canada, Hong Kong, and Japan. She has successfully negotiated contracts for Colorado companies with Holland and Great Britain. Negotiations are proceeding with Canada and seem at this time also headed for success.

The Small Business Assistance Center, in support of the Colorado Wheat Growers Association, hosted a delegation of Taiwanese on a buying trip to Colorado to purchase wheat and barley. Their visit culminated in the purchase of $13 million worth of Colorado products. The center, in conjunction with the Long-Term Credit Bank of Japan, held a seminar on campus for twenty-seven Japanese industrialists and eight of our high-tech firms to introduce them to each other and to give our firms an opportunity to propose negotiations for reverse investments into Colorado, a topic of great interest to the Japanese.

Establishing an international network continues to be a priority. All this has been accomplished within the past eight months.

Small food-processing manufacturers in the state's rural areas have a tremendous need for sales and marketing assistance. Developmental procedures, such as packaging design, product pricing structure, and identification of appropriate distribution channels are areas in which we must supply assistance if we hope to have a percentage of our state's food manufacturers reach export potential. A multifaceted approach is necessary for this project because of the enormous diversity of products our manufacturers are producing and because of the complexity of the international market place.

Solving real-life problems

Descriptions of some of the problems and solutions that our consultant has encountered at the grass-roots level follow.

Problem: A client who, with our assistance found a market for lamb offal in the United Kingdom, has a buyer interested in low-cost meat byproducts for dog food to be produced there. All major meat processors in Great Britain have contract commitments for fertilizer and low-cost animal feeds to be rendered from byproducts.

Solution: We introduced our lamb client to our buffalo client. The buffalo client has been throwing away the byproducts. If freight logistics can be worked out cost effectively—and she tells me they are—we will have a contract with the buffalo people, the lamb people, and Great Britain. Everyone will win.

Problem: A small co-op in the southwestern part of the state has 60,000 pounds of a unique bean, one that archaeologists digging in Mesa Verde found in pots long buried. An entrepreneuer in the area took these beans and over the years has grown a crop. They are presently stored in a warehouse. The client can't find a U.S buyer because of the relatively small supply available and the lack of consumer identification—and therefore appeal—of the bean.

Solution: Using U.S. Department of Commerce Census figures, we targeted four countries that were currently importing bulk beans and including bean products as a staple of their diets. We contacted brokers in the Netherlands, France, Japan, and South Africa and received a letter requesting further information from a company in the Netherlands. With our assistance, the client sent samples, product information, and a price list. We have just received a preliminary order for eighteen metric tons of these beans.

Problem: A small manufacturer of gourmet sauerkraut and applesauce has an interested buyer in Canada. However, the product needs to be kept cold and has a very short shelf life—4-6 months—which makes this product very expensive. The jar presently being used has a high incidence of breakage.

Solution: We have been working with a manufacturer to redesign the package. The client has chosen a jar with higher import potential and a corrugated carton with greater tensile strength. We have also made the necessary contact with the macrobiology lab at Colorado State University, which is going to contract with the client to develop a longer shelf life for the product.

Problem: A preliminary agreement has been made with a meat broker in

Hong Kong for buffalo stomach, commonly known as tripe. However, only 3,000 buffalo a year are slaughtered in Colorado—about 900 pounds of processed tripe—and we need at least 25,000 pounds to fulfill the contract demand.

Solution: Producers are trying to find domestic demands for Colorado buffalo that would increase the demand for prime cuts and therefore increase the number slaughtered. We have been working with the buffalo group in identifying brokers and direct outlets in the United States. We have recommended that the Colorado buffalo group contact out-of-state buffalo processors to offer to buy frozen stomachs which can then be consolidated for overseas shipment. The client would have a profitable business acting as the middleman.

We anticipate a gradual acceleration of success stories such as these in light of increasing public awareness. Even though we are in the early stages of this program, we are quite pleased with the role the University of Colorado Small Business Assistance Center has played in stimulating international trade as Colorado agricultural producers become more aware of the international market.

8

Pleasures and Pitfalls in Developing International Trade

Frank Hoy

The author is director of the Small Business Development Center of Georgia and assistant professor of management for the University of Georgia.

The Georgia Tech University International Trade Development Center (ITDC) started in 1979 as a result of a survey of Georgia businesses to find out what was occurring in international trade. The survey revealed that little was happening, and businesses were not aware of what little activity was actually underway.

It was clear there was a need for the ITDC to assist businesses with exporting—at a minimum, to help business owners and prospective owners become aware of the kinds of assistance available to them for products or services with the potential for export. I initially doubted whether the program could be viable. After all, the Department of Commerce was already involved in international trade, and there was the Department of Industry and Trade in our own State of Georgia. Wasn't enough already being done? But the more we looked, the clearer became the need for institutional assistance in international development.

Since we started the program, the demand for our services has expanded considerably. The ITDC has an extensive program established to make business owners aware of trade opportunities and to provide direct assistance.

Programs that work

We started our program conducting awareness programs, going around the state and letting business owners know what kinds of assistance were available and what kinds of opportunities existed for small businesses in international trade. We've expanded that effort with one-on-one counseling, particularly to specific industries that have tremendous export potential. We set up, under contract to the U.S. Small Business Administration, an export information system in which business clients in Georgia, or clients working through Small Business Development Centers (SBDCs) in other states, can get market information about foreign countries to determine whether there is a market for their products or services.

We have also set up exchange programs with institutions in other countries. I particularly want to point out Stirling University in Scotland, with which we have set up an exchange. We develop market information for them to use with some of their clients, and they develop market information for us to use with our clients who want to market in Europe.

Stirling University and some other programs are actively involved with entrepreneurial development in the international scene. In England, entrepreneurs are paid to participate in a program for several weeks; as a result, many of the businesses acquire an international focus. At Stirling University, the decision has been made to allocate considerable resources for specific entrepreneurs to get their businesses started.

I recently visited Babson College, which has started a Center for International Entrepreneurship Development. It offers programs that allow people involved in international trade and entrepreneurship development to "network" with one another, establish contacts, and exchange market data and information about their programs to train entrepreneurs in international trade.

In Malaysia the government is funding a program for prospective entrepreneurs to go to Canada, the United States, Great Britain, and other countries to study entrepreneurship. In fact, it is prepared to subsidize these students through a one- or two-year graduate program featuring entrepreneurship at institutions around the world so that they can develop skills they can take back to Malaysia to get their entrepreneurial firms started.

In Canada, the University of Calgary is conducting an off-campus intensive graduate program for prospective entrepreneurs and is uniting entrepreneurs with venture capitalists.

I will soon be going, with a number of other SBDC directors, to Brazil to take our models to various universities and conduct training programs, to apprise them of how our programs operate and how they have succeeded in the United States. They can pick and choose among these programs to determine what will work at their own institutions.

Pitfalls

Many current trends and programs reveal that universities are seen as playing pivotal roles in making international trade programs successful, and that there is a need for this knowledge transfer. But although there have been many successes, I must mention some of the obstacles.

One—the first and most obvious—is the value of the dollar overseas. This factor has certainly affected our ability to work with clients in Georgia. As the dollar increases in value, we find our clients encounter difficulties in international marketing of their products. A "shake-out" is involved. They find themselves at a competitive disadvantage because of the price of their products, and that obstacle is very hard for any management assistance program to overcome. But we also find that there are always opportunities—market niches—for many organizations.

International marketing tends to emphasize cultural differences around the world. One hears people say, "People are people, they are just like us wherever we go; wherever we travel we find people are the same as we are." But in international trade we don't find that to be the case. People are not the same, and if one tries to market products in foreign countries the same way as one does in the United States, one is bound to experience disaster. There are cultural elements that make marketing very different in foreign lands. We had a client come in recently who had an idea of marketing a computerized sewing machine to countries in West Africa. That might be a brilliant idea—very clearly, this is something one could envision a market for in the States. Here's a new technology that will replace a lot of hand labor, cut costs, be highly productive, and be very attractive to labor-intensive markets. But if one evaluates the cost of labor in those other markets and the technical support for any enterprise involving a computer, and if one then considers some of the political ramifications for a country that wants to make sure people have jobs and are not displaced by technology, then one realizes that this idea might work beautifully here but is not going to be viable in certain other cultures.

We also find, in working with entrepreneurs, that many people who have products with good market potential in foreign countries simply do not want to make the effort to learn how to export. Because of the strength of our economy, Americans have not made any great efforts to market to foreign countries.

We continue to find this to be true for with many of the clients and potential clients with whom we work. Mayor Young has been trying in the Atlanta area to get a pallet manufacturer to export its products. There is a tremendous market for them. He has already identified some of the market opportunities. The company president, however, does not want to do it. She says she's "too old to learn" how to do it. International marketing is too hard, there are too many problems, there are legal requirements; there are problems identifying buyers overseas, "things will get out of her control," and she just does not want to learn how to do it.

That is part of the key role management assistance organizations can play: to prevent business owners with export opportunities from having to spend years of their lives retooling to learn the international market. But the pitfall of entrepreneurs' reluctance to learn how to retool is formidable.

There are other constraints involved in international marketing. It requires intensive effort, much more than typical face-to-face consulting demands. We're finding in Georgia, however, that there is a trememdous pay-off from such effort—not only to individual business owners, but also to the state and to the nation.

The Higher Education Mission and Economic Development

9

A Policy Environment for Human Capital Development

Peter Smith

The author is Lieutenant Governor of the State of Vermont. He also serves as chairman of the board of directors of the Fund for Improvement of Postsecondary Education and as an advisory council member of the Carnegie Forum on Education and Economic Development.

Winston Churchill, as you know, had an enormous capacity for Scotch whiskey. An admirer in his office one day said, "Winston, I understand that if all the Scotch whiskey you had ever drunk in your life were poured into this office with the door shut, it would come up to here," pointing to about the height of Churchill's desk. It was a huge office, and Churchill, all 5 foot 5 inches of him, stood back and looked at the top of his desk and at the ceiling and around the office and said, "So much accomplished, so much more to do."

The higher education/business connection

This is the situation we are in with regard to making the connection between higher education and economic development, and it is unlikely that we will resolve the policy issues all at once. The nature of these issues is such that they will never be resolved because they are dynamic and are going to demand that institutions and individuals, both in higher education and in business, develop the kind of flexibility that has heretofore rarely been seen, though there are a few examples of it around today.

As a state executive, chairman of the board at the Fund for the Improvement of Postsecondary Education (FIPSE), and committee chairman at the Education Commission of the States, I would call the issue of connecting higher education and business a double cutting-edge issue. It holds enormous opportunities for us societally, educationally, and economically if it is addressed with foresight, courage, and imagination. But there is great peril for us if we fail in these tasks, because in our society now the production of techniques, knowledge, and ideas ranks equally with the manufacture of things.

A people-oriented, world-based approach

An approach to education that is going to be both *people friendly*—a term that suggests an attitude—and world based, another kind of an attitude, is more than a desirable goal. It is a social, civic, and economic necessity. Any successful policy or collection of policies must recognize the world as it is.

Our country is increasingly involved in the manufacture of ideas and processes, an incubator, if you will, for the rest of the world; in fact, different regions of our country act as incubators for ideas from other parts of the country. In my native region of New England, if you drive around, all you have to do is look at the old abandoned mill towns and you will undertand that just as we now ship computer parts and assembly business to the PACT nations in Southeast Asia and the Southern Pacific rim, the same kind of thing happened after the techniques for mass production of woolen and cotton goods were perfected by the end of the nineteenth century. It became cheaper to do that work elsewhere for a variety of reasons. In that case, we exported not to other countries but to other parts of the United States. And so it goes. I now see the whole country in the same mode. We develop processes and give them away, not always willingly—sometimes they are taken from us. But that is the nature of the international economy and the international information transfer we have today.

The new demographics

As our population ages, there are two enormously significant and unavoidable consequences. Over 80 percent of the current work force today will still be the work force in the year 2000. Nothing we do, save annihilation, is going to change that. We have to *do* something with those nonproducing people. Perhaps more compelling is the fact that with the declining traditional student population there is a steadily increasing cohort of young people whom we historically have failed in our schools, who have been failed by the institution of public education. By that I mean minorities and women. If we do not understand the consequences of continually failing to deal with those people and help them become empowered members of our society we are going to pay a heavy price.

Either we do a different and better job retraining our existing work force and educating our school-age populations, or we face the prospects, by the year 2000, of either exporting jobs or importing work force to this country. And those prospects should horrify anybody interested in human capital, education, social cohesion, or democracy, because such prospects would institutionalize, both educationally and economically, a two-tiered society for the perpetually growing underclass. The civic and social catastrophe that this would represent is clear.

But if that doesn't move you, let me quote Bud Hodgkinson, who said that the "two-tiered society won't be able to support us in the style to which we have become accustomed." We won't be able to pay for Social Security. We won't be able to pay for the kind of care we think senior citizens should have. We won't be able to run the multiple levels of government in this country if we have an increasing proportion of people who are out of the economic mainstream. So if we aren't wooed to the task by some sense of the way this country has been at its best, we can be reconciled to it by thinking about the consequences if we don't address the issues. In short, we can't afford to fail, but we may do just that—not collectively, but singly, institution by institution, and state by state. I may seem to be stating the obvious, but we must never underestimate the ability of higher education institutions to think that the bad news is intended for someone else.

An uneasy coexistence between education and work

Higher education, and education in general, has an almost uncanny ability to say, "Yes, that's right, things are getting bad," but to assume the worst is going to happen someplace else. Colleges always have a long list of reasons why every other college in the state is going to go out of business, but they are going to be just fine.

When we think about the world of education and the world of work, we must remember that the best relationships we've had historically have been, at best, an uneasy coexistence between those two worlds.

I would be stunned if things had changed since I left the field eight years ago to a point where four-year shools and upper divisions at state colleges and universities welcomed community college graduates and their credits, welcomed technical college graduates into their engineering programs, and bent over backwards to offer bridging programs that saved people time and let them learn on the job and counted that for regular college credit. These things haven't yet happened in Vermont. The intransigence of public policy makers at the state level results in an enormous waste of money. It also takes a toll in terms of human dignity and respect and human capital; it's an enormous waste. We ask people to do the same work over and over. And we can't afford to do that anymore. Somehow we've got to improve that uneasy coexistence between business and education.

We could get away with such neglect before because there was an expanding pool of young people. Employers could draw from that pool and replenish the work force. The nature of the work in general allowed us to employ people, keep them on for as long as they wanted, and then if a new job came along, hire somebody else. That was when people usually held the same jobs throughout their lives. It's not that way anymore. I think that without a major change in the way higher education institutions understand business and the products of higher education, we risk social stagnation at best, upheaval at worst, and certain economic decline. As if these pressures on higher education weren't enough (and I believe the pressure is on higher education and not on the business community), it wasn't very considerate of business to just go ahead and change without asking higher education's permission! And it was very inconsiderate of the parents in the Sixties and Seventies not to ask our permission before they decided to have fewer children! That, too, caused a lot of trouble in higher education. But the fact of the matter is that there are fewer people out there, and there's a changed mission out there, and to those two things I would add a third: the climate in which we operate has changed dramatically and produced pressure from what I will call an information-rich society.

Social justice in an information-rich society

Our institutions are organized to dispense what historically was a scarce commodity—organized information. Call it curriculum, call it lecture, but the whole model is based on the idea that you could not get the training somewhere else, so you came to college. You sat with the great men, or more recently women, and you learned from them. You went to the library and to the laboratory to get access to resources that you couldn't find anywhere else. College is still a place for those things, but all of a sudden those kinds of institutions are surrounded by an increasing flow of information that calls into question that basic teaching-learning mission that lies at the core of our self-perception. Alternate models are to higher education what paralegals, mediation, and self-representation are to the practice of law, or what the wellness movement, the home-birth movement, and the hospice movement are to hospitals and health care delivery systems.

We have created these institutions and hospitals and made them enormously expensive, enormously important, and now people are saying, "I don't want to wait till I get sick, I'm going to stay healthy." That's bad business for hospitals. It's causing a lot of trouble because they do not make as much money, and they have an economic bottom line just like anybody else. They never counted on five million Americans starting to jog regularly. Likewise, an information-rich society affects individuals, changes their patterns, and at the same time changes the patterns of consumption and use of major institutions in society. The same is true for political parties, for government, for labor unions, and for churches. And change introduces tension.

If educators do not figure out how to deal with change, if higher education doesn't understand how to unbundle and rebundle and reconfigure the human and physical and fiscal resources at their disposal, then they risk going the way of the dinosaurs. I have an image of large, ponderous beasts, air growing chilly, and the beasts thinking that if they just hunker down for a while the cold will pass. But we all know what happened. Institutions are enormously hard to change, but the task is that important and the challenge that great.

The abundance of information is changing forever the nature of choice for the individual. The traditional student, the adult learner, the employer, the small businessperson, the corporate executive—all are becoming informed consumers willing to shop for services and possibly, as in the case of John Hancock and an increasing number of other businesses, to create their own service if they are not satisfied. The abundance of information is a tremendous shock, a challenge to a society that has relied on such basic institutions as education, labor, the church, the corporate structure to carry the torch of social justice. By empowering the individual, an information-rich society is tinkering in a way that is profoundly disturbing—tinkering with a tortuously achieved balance between two fundamentally important and quite antagonistic notions in our society.

The balance of social justice

One is this strand of liberty—a very personal kind—of "I can do what I wish." That is a strong theme in the history and mythology of this country. The other strand is the notion of justice, which is a social notion, spreading resources out among groups of people in order to achieve social justice. Sometimes we get it and sometimes we lose it. An interesting way to look at American history is to see when we have had the balance between those two notions and when we haven't. But this balance in an information-rich society is going to be upset, I believe, as it affects institutions of higher education. There is no choice but to decide how to respond to that threat.

Of the seven functions described in *The Higher Education-Economic Development Connection: Emerging Roles for Public Colleges and Universities in a Changing Economy,* the human capital function, broadly defined as targeted human resource development, is the most important for several reasons.

First, the other economic development functions, such as research and technology transfer, involve the more traditional concept of contracts between or among institutions, between and among professionals. It is business that is done between new kinds of partners. But at the basic level of human capital, it does not involve people who need to learn—people who need to leave the contract with more than they had when they came, which is the primary function of education.

Those other functions, as important as they are, as complicated as they are, are easier to do because they can be negotiated at the table. That is one of the reasons we see more progress on those fronts than on basic changes in the way institutions are organized to do business. Organizational change involves social culture and mythology, organizational structure and the history, which are difficult to change.

The human capital strategy

Economic development will rise or fall on the success of the human capital strategy. Human capital strategy will or will not, depending on its success or failure, preserve our social fabric, and strengthen our civic and economic life. Time and again I have heard men and women across this country express a deep despair, turning to frustration and anger, over a system that denied their life experience, their measurable skills and the abilities they had gained outside of school (which is, by the way, statistically proven to be 90 percent of all the things we all know)—denied that they had anything of educational or economic value to society. These folks didn't want a free ride. They wanted respect for the things they had learned; they wanted respect for the persons they had become; they wanted recognition for what they knew as a base for learning more, whether on the job or in the classroom. They found in all too many cases that personnel and academic policies rewarded credentials instead of true ability. And we *can* measure the latter; we simply do not. Almost to a person, they saw colleges as gatekeepers to the market place, not as bridges to opportunity.

If colleges are really going to become adult and "business friendly," they are going to have to change the core of their nature, and play the role, for their students, of advisor, mentor, consultant, as opposed to simply instructor.

The human capital strategy is the most difficult to integrate and sustain, whether within an institutional or state policy framework. The new demographic changes make it essential that human capital strategy be the underpinning of any education, higher education, or business long-term policy.

What, then, is the proper policy climate for human capital issues today? At both the state and institutional level the same strategies will work, not just for human capital but for other economic development functions as well. We should encourage, we shouldn't regulate. We should give incentives for institutional change, not dictate. We should allow for many models that would subscribe loosely to Schumacher's appropriate-technology metaphor, and we should encourage testing and evaluating of the alternatives and encourage risk taking. Instead of rewarding the status quo, we should be searching for the right answer.

Entrepreneurial institutions are needed

The recent AASCU study on higher education and eocnomic development concludes that the most important precondition for success was entrepreneurial leadership at the presidential level, and it is absolutely right. But our policy goal should be broader. We need entrepreneurial institutions with a policy latitude and a mission range, the ability and flexibility to respond to the needs of the community around them—the people, the institutions, and the community development programs. Not at the fringe, not in a piecemeal fashion, but in comprehensive ways that commit the resources and rewards higher education has to offer to those people and to those institutions on their terms.

That means joint appointments, academic credit, financial aid, new curricula, new degree programs, assessment of prior and experiential learning, financial incentives to develop partnerships—all these must not only exist, but prosper.

At the core of it all, the appropriate policy climate will encourage an appropriate technology response for each situation. It will tolerate diversity and will recognize that for any change to be lasting in the culture of higher education, people in each institution must be actively involved in the creation of their future, because before you can integrate a solution you have to own it. When was the last time somebody told you to do something and you loved it? It was a long time ago for me. And we know when you want to make change, you have to build it in and give away some traditional sense of power, and then it will flourish in that soil.

The soil of dictatorial measures is rocky and barren; it won't nourish the kind of change we need. In this new climate institutions will survive to the extent that they become good at assessing the learning already accomplished by their new students and assessing their distinctive needs. They will also need to assess the needs of business in the surrounding community, and respond to noninstructional needs in the same way they have traditionally provided instruction on campus and performed traditional research. The idea of assessment is an essential precondition to effective instruction or an effective relationship between two organizations. It assumes sufficient resource flexibility and a policy structure to mold the education to the need—to fit into the research resources to the problem, instead of asking the learners and the businesses to fit the right higher education mold.

Many questions arise from institutions and policy makers in this kind of organization. The issues include quality control, funding, and many others. But examples of good practice for each of these kinds of models exist in this country today. The only thing that stands between any faculty or institution and doing these things is their lack of desire or their belief that it does not need doing.

I don't underestimate how enormous this chasm is. But the models of good practice do exist, and we can use them, build them, and plug them in within a year in any institution. It is the policy makers' challenge to create the attitude in institutions that leads to a climate where innovations are possible.

A Vermont example

Let me describe one set of policies at the state level in Vermont that has made an enormous difference over the last fifteen years. We have, after fifteen years, one of the most open systems of public and private higher education in the country. We achieved that by changing the environment in which our colleges and businesses work, changing the reward structure, and sharing good practices across the state. We have a statewide external associate degree program at the community college level. Statewide, people can come part time, go in, go out; students can plan their curriculum. There's no limit placed on curriculum. Over 2,000 students a year in a state of half a million people go to that type of college. A statewide, external, upper-division baccalaureate program is run by Johnson State College in the state college system. There are the same basic models and clusters all over the state in businesses, churches, and so on. A cluster—ten people—can be student-designed, approved by the faculty at Johnson State College. There is room for private institutions to participate, and other state colleges can participate, too. It allows for flow away from the campus if that's what people feel they need. In place of public and private colleges, we have statewide consortia that assess prior experiential learning on a common form for transfer to the programs mentioned above, or to any other institution that will take them.

So we have students shopping for colleges with credit for their life experience awarded by interdisciplinary, interinstitutional faculty panels in a coin that everybody understands: credits adding up to 120 that lead to a degree. Those students shopping have done more to change the behavior of some institutions in the state of Vermont than many other external forces we might have dreamed up.

We have a similar consortium that works with the business community on a forty-eight hour turnaround to broker inservice and ongoing training. Public and private institutions working together again. No turf is involved; they have worked it out. The goal is for business to walk away satisfied. We haven't gotten as sophisticated as some of the models I've heard about, and in many respects that's because there are only two places in the state where a great deal kind of sophistication would be even remotely appropriate. But the important thing is that we have that consortium.

Creating an access grid

We have a significant state commitment to adult and part-time student financial aid funded out of the general fund of the state of Vermont to meet the different, special needs of adult learners. So if you are a man or a woman who has a job (or does not have a job), outside the home, and you wish to go to school, and you need money, not for dormitories, but for day care, not for food necessarily, but for transportation, we've got a financial aid program for you. And we have a financial aid program if you are unemployed. Why in the world would a person who is unemployed, who had just fallen from what we would call loosely the lower middle class in Vermont, who might have an asset, like a house—why in the world would that person mortgage that asset at the time of maximum insecurity and anxiety to go back to school? So we tried a simple thing. We said you can take two courses. *You* decide whether they are job related and clear it with the financial aid agency. Two courses, financial aid, no means test. We figured that the self-interest of a man or a woman who has just lost a job has got to count for more, both in terms of picking appropriate education and seeing it through, than any set of regulations we could write. At the end of the first year of that program we funded it with just a little bit of money.

The results were astonishing. Over two-thirds of the people who had enrolled in that program were either continuing their education or working in the area in which they took their first course. A powerful connection arose between these students—the clients—and their sense of where they wanted to take their lives. And the institution became the servant. The experience was just extraordinary.

Think of the manpower records. Think of the Comprehensive Employment Training Act (CETA). Think of the money we've spent in this country trying to achieve that, because we didn't believe that people would make some of those connections for themselves, or we didn't have the policies or the strategies in place. We have a business-higher education research partnership at the state university. We have a new venture capital corporation. We're beginning to work on some of those other partnerships.

This policy structure allows our institutions to serve special needs in mainstream ways. And that's what we've got to learn to do. It also gives adult learners multiple entry points into the system without any penalty. They can come and go. They can participate at the certificate level and come back at the degree level. There is no penalty for that. The system is built around them. By creating incentives for individuals and institutions throughout the state, we have created an access grid that serves the needs of both business and higher education institutions that want to change, and one that clearly serves the needs of the men and women of the State of Vermont who need an education. Fifteen years ago Vermont had one adult program. Now there are more than ten spread around the state. These are adult, postsecondary degree programs throughout the private sector in higher education as well as the public sector. In short, this policy climate has enriched the mix, created incentives, and literally changed the environment in which students, colleges, and businesses live. It has also changed the face of opportunity and economic development in our state.

In this policy environment, unemployment in Vermont has been just a jot above 4 percent for the last year—and we haven't been above 6 percent in three years.

"Pull" strategies change the climate

No one can resolve the policy issues because they are by their nature dynamic. But consider what I call the push-pull strategy. Any strategy or policy you design to *push* institutions into new behavior is almost always doomed to fail—or at best to be marginally successful, because people don't take pushing well. *Pull* strategies are the ones that change the climate. They are policies that create, if you will, an oxygen-rich atmosphere. If you're after combustion, create a policy climate with incentives for figuring out how to serve adults in a way that serves both them and the institution well. It makes great sense to work with business because then everybody wins. That's the kind of policy climate that encourages diversity and changes the environment in which students and institutions operate.

At the institutional level, we need policies that promote what I call the "assessment behavior." Before allocating resources, think about what the problem is, about fitting education to the need, not vice versa, about developing the appropriate educational technology to serve the needs of business and the emerging student population. Most of all, think about institutions and individuals becoming entrepreneurs in the field of human capital development.

10

The Responsibilities of Public Universities for Economic Development

Thomas Stauffer

The author is chancellor of the University of Houston-Clear Lake. He also serves as vice-chair of the Texas Council on Science and Technology and chairs the Committee on Advanced Technology for Texas Economic Development.

My state of Texas and my city of Houston are learning what states and cities in the Northeast, Midwest, and Northwest have also been learning in recent years: economic development is terribly important. The reason for this Texas discovery has been well reported. Recently the *Wall Street Journal* ran a front-page article entitled, "Oil Recession Plunges Houston Into a State of Mental Depression," and a recent *U.S. News and World Report* cover showed a cowboy boot slipping on a pool of oil. Texas is economically exposed through its oil and gas industry when members of the Organization of Petroleum Exporting Countries drive down the world price of hydrocarbons, as they have done lately. It is no wonder that my chief task as vice-chair of the Texas Science and Technology Council is to prepare a document, requested by Governor Mark White, entitled, "Strategies for the New Texas Economy."

Diversifying the Texas economy

In Houston, and throughout Texas, the most magical words now are *economic diversification*. Although Texas is a strong, free-enterprise state, its economy has been propped up since the early 1970s by a classic, international price-fixing scheme. When that scheme collapsed, suffering in the "oil patch" began. In my city today, the newly formed Houston Economic Development Council has developed a strategic plan through the year 2000, which stresses not only the importance of the energy industry, but also space commercialization, medicine/biotechnology, international trade, and the tourism/convention business: *that* is economic diversification. Recently, in a kind of metaphor for Houston's Strategic Plan, the director of the Johnson Space Center became the president of the Houston Chamber of Commerce.

Remembering the bumper sticker that appeared in Texas in the 1970s, "Let the Yankees Freeze in the Dark," I am not asking sympathy for my state. In fact, Texas has now been galvanized into action, and I am personally optimistic about the future of the state's economy and spirit.

To colleagues from the Frost and Rust Belt states, the Texas dilemma will sound familiar. Events go in cycles, of course, and it is now Texas's turn to take a hit. In fact, Texas is a microcosm of threats to the national economy posed by large budget and trade deficits, in addition to substantial job dislocations. The challenges Texans face are challenges Americans face nationwide. Everyone must be concerned about economic development and industrial competitiveness, and there is broad opinion supporting this view. We know that we cannot continue indefinitely with our deficit ways, and we all sense, even if we do not know the precise answers, that something needs to be done and done resolutely.

Public universities and public responsibilities

Public universities, I assert, do have a responsibility for economic development. This is part of the public trust through which state institutions are supported; it is a natural extension of a public university's basic functions. If public universities nationwide have not figured out a role for themselves in this national picture, they have simply not tried hard enough. Indeed, many private institutions have taken up their own economic development responsibilities, although, by their natures, it is perhaps more of an optional part of their missions than is the case with public institutions.

Higher education in the United States follows two basic traditions: independence from governmental control, which implies a closer relationship with the private sector, and voluntary service to meet societal needs. Economic development is only the latest variation on the voluntary service theme.

Both of these traditions distinguish U.S. higher education from that found in the Soviet Union, Europe, Japan, and elsewhere, although there is movement worldwide toward closer university collaboration to meet overall economic objectives. In Japan, for example, where a traditional distance has existed between universities and business concerns, the establishment of "science universities" has encouraged more cooperation. In the Soviet Union, party review boards have been active in examining the curricula of universities to see whether they mesh adequately with local economic needs. Academic freedom certainly does not exist there as we know it, but the economic linkage is an interesting phenomenon. In Common Market countries, the distance between universities and business/industry has narrowed considerably in the last decade from the traditional model of mutual aloofness.

In the United States, the history of American higher education has largely evidenced movement away from the classical European traditions of education toward the "practical arts." The classical model has faded gradually. In 1827, after much debate, faculty members at Yale announced they had no responsibility in their scholarship for practical aspects of the world. This set the pattern for the next several decades until such reformers as President Francis Wayland of Brown University began to make contrary recommendations. In the 1850s, he proposed that the Brown curriculum be made more practical, perhaps echoing West Point's involvement in the development of American railroads and other more modest involvements elsewhere.

The roots of the business/economic development-higher education connection in the United States can be traced to traditions of Jacksonian democracy and the rise of American industrial society. Largely, until the 1850s, colleges were agrarian in nature and looked mostly to the past. Whereas the Yale report called for the primacy of the classics as the basis for a balanced mind, Wayland inquired, "What could Virgil and Horace and Homer and Demosthenes, with little mathematics and natural philosophy, contribute to developing the untold resources of the continent?" It was a good and reasonable question. So impressed were the Rhode Island General Assembly and the Providence Asociation of Mechanics and Manufacturers that they supported Wayland's various reforms and helped raise $125,000 for the purpose—possibly the first grant from American business in support of academic change at an institution of higher learning.

Although Wayland's reforms largely failed at Brown, he proved merely to be a step ahead of his time, as the reform movement picked up speed around the time of the Civil War. The Morrill Act of 1862 is the watershed of this period, but the appointment of Charles Eliot as Harvard's president in 1869 and Johns Hopkins's pledging of his fortune in Baltimore and Ohio Railway stock in 1867 to a university alerted the higher education establishment that fundamental change was afoot. By 1900 the old order was being shouldered aside, except in some isolated colleges, by the rise of science and industry. In the twentieth century, milestones included inauguration of cooperative education programs at the University of Cincinnati in 1906, the establishment of 207 two-year (mostly vocational) colleges by 1921, and the founding of the Business-Higher Education Forum in 1978. With such movement, the next step to economic development was a short one.

Perhaps the best summary of these developments was recorded in 1953 when the Chesapeake and Ohio Railway Company sponsored a "Conference on Industry-College Relations," chaired by Milton Eisenhower, the president of Pennsylvania State University who later became president of Johns Hopkins University. Convened at the Greenbrier Hotel, participants concluded,

> The need for better understanding through closer industry-college relations is a matter of national importance. While a few . . . institutions . . . have developed [a strong relationship with business and industry] . . . most colleges are working in limited areas. . . . College administrative offices take a lively interest in plans to improve relations with industry. Many, however, are still verbalizing. Many fail to see obvious opportunities; few have thought beyond the obvious aspects of the relationships. Industry has little grasp of the totality of its dependence on educational institution[s]. . . . Industry rarely initiates a relationship with a college except when it requires [something] specific—mainly personnel, instruction, or research. Colleges . . . have little understanding of the benefits to education that might accrue from a closer relationship. Industry is humble; colleges are shy. The problem is complex. It is now obscured by cliches.

By the 1980s, some change has come about, but the contemporaneous appeal of this conclusion from the Eisenhower report rings true. Industry is now less humble and universities are certainly less shy. Yet mutually beneficial collaboration between business and higher education, especially on matters of economic development, is still being formed, although the linkage is more natural than might be supposed.

How business and academe can work together

American business and American higher education, especially since World War II, have entered into a reasonable partnership. Business people are trustees of colleges and universities. They are alumni and parents and students. They serve on advisory bodies. They participate in the Conference Board, the Joint Committee on Economic Education, the Business-Higher Education Forum, the Council for Financial Aid to Education, and other collaborative groups. Corporate and campus employees have contact through professional societies, business and technical training programs, job recruitment, summer visitations and exchanges, and business executives-in-residence programs. Interaction occurs in plant visits, scholarships, cooperative education, lifelong learning and career changes, internships, colloquia and courses, curricular materials, contractual arrangements, and philanthropy, among other examples. There is joint activity through consultancies and speakers, health and research programs, education of corporate employees, and management and advice. Businesses play a prominent role in the debate on the value of liberal arts as compared with vocational/technical curricula. Higher education has been a source of fundamental research, expertise, and trained manpower, and business has provided the productive margin that has permitted colleges and universities to prosper. Studies from the Brookings Institution have indicated that about 75 percent of the improvement in the American standard of living since World War II has come from education and research, thus providing the private sector with its own productive margin.

Because the free-market economy and academic freedom have similar roots, there would seem to exist a reasonable basis for fraternization. Yet clearly, each sector has a distinct point of view. Private enterprise fulfills its primary function when it makes a socially responsible profit; universities do so when they are sources of learning and criticism. Sometimes these two functions conflict, and misunderstandings may develop. The Vietnam War era is an obvious example. But as Professor John Dunlop of Harvard, former Labor Secretary and advisor to two presidents, has observed, differences between the sectors need to be recognized and respected so that coalition building around a common agenda can take place.

Historical development of the partnership

Since the early 1970s, interconnections between corporation and campus have been growing, in part, from mutually enlightened self-interest. Students have demanded more relevance of the curriculum to their career interests; college and university presidents have asked for more help, financial and in-kind. Corporate executives, more and more frequently the products of graduate education themselves, have shown appreciation for the powerful societal roles universities can play in teaching, research, and public service. This coalition has been fostered by such influencial phenomena as global interdependence, mass opinion, governmental regulation, technology, and what has been called the postindustrial American economy. In short, powerful forces abide around which to unite. Furthermore, as Dunlop has concluded, "America is a society of coalitions, and both business and higher education need friends in society."

Today, business/industry-higher education's connectedness is the rule more than the exception. A recent study by the American Association of State Colleges and Universities, for example, found that half of the public institutions surveyed declared themselves engaged in some aspect of economic development. This activity may be manifest as involvement with economic education and analysis or through human resource and industrial agreements involving courses, technical assistance to small businesses, industrial parks, business incubators, and other such measures. In 1983, the Office of Technology Assessment, an adjunct of Congress, identified 150 programs nationwide relating to these themes; probably at least 500 such programs could be identified today.

In February 1986, the Higher Education Panel of the American Council on Education surveyed 1,933 institutions about their ties to the business community. Almost all institutions said they had some business ties; 85 percent said they had business people serving on various advisory panels. In this survey, 75 percent of colleges and universities received equipment loaned or donated from businesses; 63 percent had scholarship or loan programs sponsored by the private sector; 65 percent received such research moneys; 60 percent offered courses on business premises; and 44 percent reported having developed direct partnerships with state/regional agencies to foster economic development.

Determining future directions

For the most part, business-higher education relationships have largely concerned what would most benefit universities, because universities consider themselves in greatest need. But in terms of economic development, the real question is what universities can do for the areas they serve. If a rising tide raises all ships, then regional economic development can be of direct assistance to universities by producing more students, more activity of all kinds, and a larger constituency.

Economic development concerns not only a university's external relationships but its internal activities as well. For instance, to effect full participation in regional business activity, it would behoove universities to pursue program review, rigorous promotion and tenure standards, and new research programs sensitive to the environments they serve. Although some experiments fail and unrealistic expectations can exist, the benefits of such commitment often far outweigh the consequences. And universities become immersed in the economic development and prosperity of their service areas. Although universities are responsible for teaching, research, and public service, economic development can become a new function that increases their value to society.

Universities can reap important advantages from economic development. It is certainly good politics in that it builds a partial justification for the university; it is also good economics and demographics in that it improves the strategic environment for the university. Adding such a function permits faculty members and students to participate in many beneficial, if external, activities on behalf of the university. The university's leadership generally will have access to levels of state and regional policy making probably otherwise unattainable. Thus, the university's mission is widened to include not only economic development activity but also technology transfer and applied research.

To make all this possible, the chief executive officer of the university must take the lead; he or she must be assertive and be willing to take some criticism. In addition, there are many other things a university can do to enhance its profile in economic development. Meetings can be convened, data bases can be developed, organizations for economic development and other activities can be established, university programs can be made more responsive to local needs, industrial research parks can be developed, and many other projects can be pursued.

Given the current trends toward a more service-oriented, technology-based economy, university involvement in economic development is essential. If people are to believe in this enterprise, word should be carried to the various institutional constituencies. A great deal of movement has occurred in recent years in higher education in support of economic development, and I expect such activity to be one of the important innovations of American higher education in this century.

11

Higher Education and Economic Development: A Symbiotic Relationship

J. Wade Gilley

The author is senior vice president at George Mason University. He has directed development of the George Mason Institute, a nationally recognized corporate relations program.

In 1948 the chairman of the education committee of the United States Chamber of Commerce was a man named Thomas Boushall, an innovative banker who originated bank credit cards and consumer installment credit. Boushall believed strongly that it behooved American business to support high-quality public education and be willing to help pay for it.

To prove his point, Boushall commissioned a study of educational quality and business activity among a broad array of American communities. The study revealed that a strong business community always accompanied a strong, high-quality, and well-supported educational system. Which was cause and which effect was not proven in the study: the relationship appeared symbiotic.

In other words, it is in the interest of business to promote, support, and even insist on a strong educational system. Likewise, it is in the educational system's interest to work with business to achieve mutual goals. This simple axiom, yet complex relationship, has been essential to the economic development of America ever since the beginnings of the industrial revolution. American higher education has grown and been shaped by a nation growing—both economically and in population.

Historical roots of the collaboration

For example, our excellent system of land-grant colleges was established in direct response to the flowering of the industrial revolution and rapidly growing population. The original curricula of these institutions—agriculture and mechanical arts—were designed specifically to train technical personnel for industry. Out of this educational experiment have come the scientists and engineers who produced the economic wonder of the industrial age.

The land-grant experiment has produced some of American's best and most distinctive universities. These very comprehensive institutions are still unique in their support of economic development. For example, that large and sophisticated agricultural extension service complete with research and experiment stations is the technology transfer model for the nation.

In an upwardly spiraling process, increased business development demanded greater expertise, while educational research fueled technological expansion. As the nation continued to develop, a high school education became increasingly important, and normal schools, state colleges, and regional universities were born. They are now major resources for their regions. Similarly, after World War II, increased public access to higher education and postsecondary technical education became essential to the nation's economy. From thence sprang the community college. Finally, the national investment in science and technology transfer education after Sputnik was largely responsible for the current international leadership position of the United States in science and technology.

Now the nation again finds itself in a great transitional period: the continuing shift from the industrial age, with machines amplifying muscle power, to the information age, with machines amplfying brain power. Other changes include the shift to a global economy, with labor-intensive jobs moving overseas, and the redistribution of jobs within the U.S.A., from the traditional industrial centers to a more even geographic distribution.

These changes have promoted competition among the regions and states. Consequently, governors and legislators are undertaking educational initiatives in the name of economic development. There is less interest in general funding increases and more interest in funding special initiatives that focus on economic development and target improvements in quality. Recently, a university vice president said, "It seems that the only way we can get new money from the legislature is for initiatives, and business-university projects are the priority."

This, too, is not all new. In C. P. Snow's classic, *The Masters,* written in 1952 and set in 1937, a fictional college at Cambridge is confronted by a potential benefactor who wants to pull the college into a posture supportive of economic development. The book, which concentrates on the selection of a new master, has a substory about the courting of a potential benefactor—a certain industrialist named Sir Horace. It seems that the college wanted (as we all do) a general-purpose (no-strings-attached) benefaction for a new building or for improving the status quo. However, Sir Horace, thinking ahead to a possible war and what that might mean to the Commonwealth and the economy of the British Isles, wanted a benefaction to stimulate the college to produce more graduates in science and engineering. He believed that technology would be important to England's economic future. Near the end of the book, Sir Horace gave the college an endowment of 120,000 pounds—in 1927, equivalent to about $400,000—to be divided into six fellowships: four for science and technology, one to support the work of a specific professor, and one for the faculty to use for "balance." As usual, the college not only accepted the gift but quickly turned its attention to its utilization.

At least three truths emerge from this discussion hitherto:

1. As America has grown and developed culturally and economically over the past hundred years, its educational system has also grown and developed, in something of a symbiotic relationship. This interrelationship is our national heritage.

2. In the new, rapidly emerging economy, higher education's responsibility is more critical than ever before. In fact, if the tremendous resources of our colleges and universities cannot be mustered in support of the knowledge economy, the nation is truly "at risk."

3. Colleges and universities have always responded to economic incentives offered by benefactors—whether they be state or federal government, or the private sector. We work our way through the questions of autonomy and purpose to a solution acceptable to the public and the academy.

Current trends

However, there is a significant difference in the colleges of this era. That difference is suggested by statistics: in the past, major economic changes have been accompanied by major growth in the potential college-age population. Not only did existing institutions grow and develop, but new classes of institutions emerged in direct response to economic and demographic changes. Today, no new class of institution is likely to arise because of the stabilizing population. Existing institutions must bear the total responsibility for reacting to an even more fundamental change in the economy. State initiatives and policies, benefactors from the private sector, and the genetic inclination of institutions to respond to economic needs will ensure the acceptance of this responsibility and the subsequent institutional changes.

Some colleges, in special locations with entrepreneurial leadership, will see potential for major institutional advancement in supporting economic development. They will prove aggressive in their quest. In fact, new universities or a new class of institutions may emerge from existing colleges and universities.

Institutional involvement in economic development is now imperative. The question for college and university leaders is not why or whether, but rather how their institution should participate to its best advantage.

Approaches to involvement

As institutions assess their invovlement in regional, and even statewide, economic development, they should take a strategic view. Based on the author's experiences in higher education and extensive research, the following strategies are suggested as models for regional universities:

1. *Commitment of the university president.* More than any other institutional staff members, chief executive officers set the standard. They have, or should have, the key business and industry contacts. Their position comes with an admission card (entry) to executive suites in the private sector and government. Without interest and active support from the the president, others in the university can only do so much, go only so far.

A liberal arts dean from a major established university assumed the presidency of a new regional university. The region of this institution was and is large, sophisticated, and growing. But the university's academic program, faculty, quality, and strategic vision were indistinguishable from those of a dozen other regional universities. And, other than a fledgling business school, it had few programs supporting its business community.

This new president searched for unique regional resources and needs, accepted every opportunity to meet with community groups and leaders (and even created others), and brought people on campus to engage in discussions about what type of university the region really needed. Within three years, he had generated a broad regional consensus.

The strategic plan for the university evolved with four development goals. First was rededication to a high-quality liberal arts education. Second was tying specific programs of instruction, research, and service to the needs of the larger community. Third was making the university the cultural focal point for the entire region. And fourth was targeting a high-quality program to attract national attention and thereby foster community pride in the university.

This broad-based, yet focused, explainable, and understandable strategic mission has proven highly successful. The four strategic points have been mutually supportive; broad enough for most academic departments to find a complementary role for themselves; provided a foundation for both short- and long-term planning and budgeting, given local community leaders and state policy makers a sense that the university knows what it is doing; dramatically accelerated private and governmental support; and begun to garner a measure of national attention.

2. Consideration of economic development in institutional strategic planning. One of the fastest-growing practices in American higher education, popularized by George Keller and others, is strategic planning. A systematic approach to developing a strategic plan includes environmental scanning—that is, examining those external conditions and forces that may affect an institution. For regional universities, there is no question that both the short- and long-term viability of the local economy will be important to their growth and development. Most public universities have the capacity to enhance economic activity in their service regions.

Last year, at Carnegie Mellon University (CMU), two civic leaders told the author that CMU "is Pittsburgh's greatest economic asset." The strategic plan for CMU shaped by president Richard Cyert has resulted in a research institution with substantial economic spinoff. The university's promise has made the city a magnet for certain kinds of industry.

But universities other than traditional research and engineering institutions can also become major forces in the economic development of their region. Examples include George Mason, Central Florida, and Wright State universities and the University of Texas in Dallas and San Antonio.

In each of these regional universities, the institution reached out to its business community looking for a true partnership—one as much business centered as university centered. And in each case, the business community responded positively and enthusiastically. These institutions immediately acquired more political muscle in their state capitals. As previously stated, a state's economy is critical to legislators and governors, especially existing, thriving business and industry.

3. Assessment of industry's expectations of regional universities. Contrary to conventional wisdom, the transfer of technology from universities is not the primary service American businesses want from their institutions of higher education, local or otherwise. The leading-edge, high-technology corporations are generating more technological advances than all but a handful of universities. When asked why he chose a site close to the University of Texas-Austin for his new research corporation, MCC, Admiral Bobby Inman said, "Because I wanted priority access to high-quality graduates in computer sciences and engineering." The critical need of most American businesses is for *productive personnel.* They want people with specific skills, but they also want broadly educated college graduates who, in the words of one high-technology CEO, "can think, write, and speak, and can adapt in the years ahead."

Business and industry are also interested in other services universities can provide—for example, faculty expertise in automation systems, developing business plans, continuing education for employees, involvement in cooperative education activities, and can adapt in the years ahead."

4. *Organization for support of business and economic development that is straightforward and simple.* In the history of American higher education, the prevailing reaction to new and uncertain requirements has been to set up a separate organizational unit and make the new activity its exclusive domain. Although small business development centers, incubator facilities, extension services, research parks, and evening programs may require their own staffs, a comprehensive, shared approach is the appropriate organizing strategy for a university committed to supporting regional economic development.

As indicated earlier, a dedicated president is essential. In addition, there should be: (1) coordinating responsiblity assigned to a vice president close to the president and one who can devote one-third of his or her time to the effort for a protracted period of time—say, two or three years; (2) an industry advisory board assigned to assist the president in overall industry strategic planning and to help identify and carry out productive collaborations; (3) an internal council composed of faculty members and administrators who, as a group, develop policy and ensure communications and who individually carry a specific responsibility in the university's interaction with business; and (4) organizational units assigned specific programmatic responsibilities.

The appropriate approach to university-business liaison is matrix management. At an institution widely recognized for its economic development activities, staff members from admissions, cooperative education, continuing education, alumni relations, and the business and engineering schools, serve as a business liaison council. Working part time (less than 10 percent of their time), each member of this group accepted responsibility to make contact with and visit five different businesses three times per year. This liaison council meets quarterly on campus to share information, develop materials, and plan strategy. Together they have developed presentation and information-gathering techniques. Each person represents the entire university to each company, and their counterparts in the business community have a reliable, responsive contact at the university when needed. After each contact, the university staff members fill out a simple report via electronic mail, which becomes part of a data base and is shared immediately. Twice a year, industry contacts are invited to campus for breakfast and orientation.

This program, with a modest investment in time on the part of seven people on campus, has established an extensive and productive institutional relationship with thirty-five regional businesses.

5. *Affiliated nonprofit corporations that spearhead major entrepreneurial activities.* A quasiuniversity, nonprofit organization has proven to be a major force for economic development in several states. The universities of Central Florida and South Florida have effectively used educational foundations, their private local arms, to acquire land, develop research parks, and enter joint ventures—all resulting in exciting economic development and enhanced university resources.

At George Mason University (VA), the educational foundation has been involved in a number of entrepreneurial activities, including land deals. Of particular interest and success is a university/private-sector partnership—the Capitol Connection. Some ten years ago, the foundation filed for and received licenses for eight ITFS channels. Later, after deregulation, the Capitol Connection received funds from a venture group on the West Coast, and a specialized television service was created for Washington, D.C. This venture has had several results: profits for the university, increased business activity and employment, new services for the city, and involvement of the faculty and students in a unique venture.

6. *University encouragement of faculty and staff members to take the initiative and act entrepreneurially.* Small businesses spinoffs from faculty research or other expertise and becoming common in American higher education. At George Mason University, over thirty faculty members have formed their own companies. The results include consulting and personal service companies, a national-circulation higher education newsletter, a software package for assessing the viability of bills introduced in Congress, video materials on teaching effective writing, and several different specialized microcomputers.

In five of these cases, George Mason has invested, in the form of release time, facilities, and cash, in the venture for a future share of the company. Two of these ventures are already paying off for the university.

Perhaps the most important strategy a university can use is to create an environment that encourages faculty members to take initiatives, act entrepreneurially, and be willing to take risks. As the information age continues, America's single greatest resource may well be the brainpower of its college and university faculty members.

Responsibilities and benefits

During the past twenty-five years, the brightest citizens have had an unprecedented opportunity to pursue advanced degrees. Some 90 percent of all Ph.D. degrees ever awarded have been earned during the last twenty years. The median age of this group, representing over 500,000 Americans, is 40-45 years—or approaching the peak of adult productive powers.

Further, this critical mass of highly educated persons is influenced by the megatrends well documented by John Naisbitt—entrepreneurship, individualism, and so forth. Faculty members with these credentials represent a huge investment by the nation and must be utilized. Universities must discover ways to free up this explosive potential, to encourage faculty members to bring their ideas to economic fruition.

Involvement in economic as well as cultural development of a region is a part of the responsibility of a regional university. It is part of the historic development of America and its universities and will be even more important as the world continues to move into an information age characterized by increased international trade competition.

Regardless of location, size, or condition, regional universities can mount active support for economic development. The endeavor takes leadership, commitment, and planning. But the payoff can be extraordinary. And why shouldn't it? After all, the story of America is a tale of a symbiotic relationship between the economy and culture of a nation and its system of higher education.

12

The Power of the People in Community Economic Development

Catherine A. Rolzinski

The author consults nationwide on higher education and the economy and was former program officer with the Fund for the Improvement of Postsecondary Education (FIPSE) and former deputy director of the Center for Education and Manpower Resources, Inc.

As colleges and universities prepare to examine or reexamine their roles and relationships to economic development, one of the key areas demanding attention is community development. Different kinds of communities with different traditions, missions, and perceptions need to form or consider forming partnerships to address problems raised by the nation's rapidly changing economy.

Having been involved in this field for at least a dozen years, the author was not surprised to note in *The Higher Education-Economic Development Connection: Emerging Roles for Public Colleges and Universities in a Changing Economy,* prepared by SRI International for AASCU, that

> 47 percent of public, four-year higher education institutions responding reported playing a significant role in the economic development of their service area, and 46.2 percent said they engaged in occasional activity related to economic development. Only 23.4 percent of them had undertaken a formal examination of their role in economic development.

The report addresses what higher education institutions have been doing in partnerships with businesses and other economic development connections and how they have been doing it. Important information and an array of past and current practice is presented, but to appreciate fully the issues involved in higher education's role in community economic development, one must also recognize a significant, unrecognized "who" missing from the report.

From an educational perspective, the missing "who" might be too obvious: the *recipients* of the education tied to economic development.

- Who are the people who identify with and reside in these communities that need to be economically developed?
- How do colleges and universities gain credibility with communities?
- How can community-based, grass-roots organizations provide a unique role to assist higher education in responding to the country's changing economic needs?
- What happens to learners in the new college-business partnerships?
- Do the partnership programs really provide adult learners with what they need to become more productive workers and effective citizens in their communities?

Communities of people in changing economies

Economic development can be defined as the creation of new wealth through the use of money, markets, manpower, materials, and management—the "five M's" of economic development theory. Community development is the planning and implementation of programs to improve the social qualities of life within a given community. The term *community economic development* refers to planning and implementing programs to improve the economic well-being of people within their social context. Getting to know a community or doing a needs assessment of a community is considered standard practice in designing economic plans and strategies. But just what is a "community"?

The word *community* comes from the Latin *communis* or "common." For purposes herein, "community" refers to a group of people who share perceptions, as in citizens living together in a smaller social unit within a larger one and having interests, work, tastes, ownership, or participation in common. Bonding from shared ethnicity or cultural heritage and values is often a strong force with community identification.

Why all this concern about definitions? Common and frequent usage of a word like "community" inures people to its meaning so that without really intending to do so, they see other people's situations through their own sense of community. With such varying perceptions, tremendous barriers can arise.

In our own communities we know what to expect and how to react. We know how to get things done. We know the structures and how to work within them and around them. We know how to dress, talk, socialize—we know what is appropriate. All of these known elements provide us with a certain degree of security. We know what we have in common with others in our communities. Academicians have their perceptions of the higher education community, the business community, and the community of unemployed or dislocated adult workers. If those of us in higher education are to collaborate successfully in economic development endeavors, we ought to look beyond the demographics to the people living in economically depressed situations. We must face the challenge of relinquishing our sense of comfort and security of place in order to try to experience people's differences and circumstances in their communities as they experience them. This process lays the groundwork for effective community economic development.

Who are the prospective new learners in the higher education-economic development ventures? Most of them are adults. Many are in their thirties, forties, and fifties and may have been working in and identifying with a particular kind of industry—such as steelworking, logging, coal mining, farming—for most of their lives. Their work has been more than just a job: it has been a lifestyle. Within each of these industries the workers have a sense of belonging, as in the "farm community" and the "logging community," with a special social life, organizations, pace, and seasonal functions.

One of the most important notions of community boils down to interdependence. Despite opposing forces, Americans seek a sense of community and have difficulty facing up to a change in lifestyle. In the Northwest the majority of workers in the timber industry have stayed on long after their jobs have ended. Against great odds, steelworkers are organizing to try to reopen closed plants and run them themselves. Many displaced or soon-to-be displaced adult workers read the papers and hear the news that their way of life is threatened, but deep inside they do not believe it. They spend a long time denying that their way of life is really coming to a close. Denial is a common stage in the process of facing death, and it is no different when it comes to the death of a lifestyle, a job, and a community.

Recently unemployed and displaced workers are often proud people who have gained a tremendous amount of knowledge and skills that seem to have no current use. After raising families, serving their community and country, acquiring property, and handling finances, these adults confront the prospect of education as a possible means to a new way of life. What do they know of the higher education community? For many of them it is more remote than a foreign country. Some never finished high school or finished it many years ago. The "university" or the "college" is often perceived as a place where others outside their peer group went. Clearly, higher education is an unknown entity to the majority of the unemployed, and people tend to fear the unknown.

Issues confronted by higher education in addressing community economic development

Each college or university is in a different stage of involvement with economic development, and each faces its own particular economic and demographic conditions; however, there are a number of concerns that institutions hold in common. As they consider community economic development, they most likely have to confront some hard questions about interpretation of institutional mission, tradition, placement and legitimacy of job-related courses, faculty reactions, styles of teaching, new groups of learners, appropriate course content and pedagogy, and financial risks.

One community economic development issue often overlooked is power. Power overshadows the other issues and is an important factor in realistic community development and education. For those of us engaged in community development and higher education, power has two aspects. One is our power, not only as we perceive it, but also as it is perceived by those for whom we work and as it affects our relationships with those to whom we may always be outsiders. The second is higher education's power vis-a-vis the communities of people with economic problems. Power plays unfold in each community's struggle to be perceived as it desires. To some degree, allowing a community to be perceived as it perceives itself can threaten the community groups deemed more powerful by the larger society. It is in this struggle that credibility can suffer, and when this happens the greatest loss is to the people who could have benefited from appropriate learning to overcome their economic circumstances.

As higher education confronts the challenges of community economic development, a new student population is being served. Adults, most of whom are or have been in the work force, represent a new direction for most institutions. For many institutions, it is the first time they have a group of learners who are mature, experienced, and looking for educational programs responsive to their employment needs. With the backgrounds these new students bring to higher education, they tend to respond to a kind of pedagogy different from higher education approaches. Appropriate pedagogy includes a more active and participatory learning, a style not usually encouraged by most faculty members.

The appearance of the new learner population raises organizational issues. Most higher education programs addressing economic development are "on the margin" within their institutions. They tend to be located in offices or centers that are peripheral to the main curricular or educational units. They usually operate entirely or partly on soft money and remain on the fringe of the institution's educational programs. Furthermore, higher education institutions grow concerned about compromising their central mission when these programs become central. If economic development continues to be perceived as a threat to higher education's mission and revenues, true legitimacy may never be achieved.

As colleges and universities redefine their missions or increase emphasis on economic development, they face the issue of forming partnerships or some type of collaborative arrangements with business, organized labor, government, and community organizations. At its most basic level, partnership involves at least a part of a single educational community working with a single business community, adult community, or labor community. At its most advanced level, collaboration involves many organizational communities. Pressures on institutional mission is a constant consideration in any of these partnership formations. With the added lure of financial benefit, it is difficult at times to keep educational value to learners and appropriate contributions to communities on track.

Another aspect of power arises when colleges and universities participate in community economic development and must consider the range of learner needs. The educational challenge is to empower people and/or organizations with skills from basic literacy to complex scientific and technological abilities and to impart a level of education that enables them to handle future economic and job changes.

Community-based organizations as viable bridges between higher education and effective community development

If we as educators are to engage in community economic development, we ought to consider that the communities we hope to serve may hold the glasses through which we can see our direction together.

Cooperating with existing community-based organizations and identifying the "right" community leaders can be the best approaches to bridging communities of people who need improved economic opportunities with the higher education institutions that want to provide that service. Most community-based organizations are involved in some kind of community education. Other common characteristics include:
- serving the community via a grass-roots approach,
- identifying with forms of learning not identified with traditional higher education,
- emphasizing function more than form in education and training programs,
- practicing a democratic process devoted to local community improvement.

Perceptions of community-based organizations can bewilder outsiders because of their diversity and the intensity of their ideologies. Many community leaders have a bias against higher education, and traditional educators have their own biases toward civic groups. These leaders often feel that higher education institutions do no recognize and appreciate their unique differences and cannot develop and deliver education appropriate to their particular community needs. On the other hand, traditional educators rarely have had the training or the organizational support to conduct community-based education. Because each group comes from such disparate communities and attempts on both sides have often been limited and superficial, suspicion often prevails.

It is important to remember that every community is different and to avoid the "I'm the expert" approach. Taking time to find the "right" person in the community or community organization is worth the effort because of the trust and credibility it fosters. Using community citizens as resources can bridge the gap between the educational institution and the community because they can represent the interests of both parties. Likewise, when a prerequisite advisory committee is formed, the important question to guide the membership is not who but what—what parts of the community, higher education, and business need to be represented?

For those higher education institutions and community organizations that have learned to appreciate each other, there has been real progress toward effective and lasting community economic development. Education institutions have a tradition of being well-suited to explore ways of stating problems and of collecting and examining relevant data, theories, and explanations that might effect policy change. Community organizations have examined the problems, theories, and data in terms of their uniqueness as they relate to a particular group, at a certain time and place, and in a framework of appropriate action. These two perceptions reinforce, in turn, perceptions of mutually exclusive domains. Why, however, cannot education's tools of research be shared with communities to empower them to participate in researching their own needs?

The author visited two rural economic development projects currently operating and effectively involving their communities. First, in the Southeast, is the Highlander Research and Education Center in New Market, Tennessee. The project is developing a participatory research and education process that enables residents of rural Appalachian communities to confront more effectively the effects of their changing economy on their collective and individual lives. The project develops models of cooperation between local higher education institutions and grass-roots community groups to meet community and individual needs resulting from changes in the economy (coal and textiles). It also develops an alternative economic curriculum to enhance the ability of these rural residents to address changing economic conditions on an ongoing basis.

In response to the declining timber industry, the University of Idaho designed a computer literacy program for rural adults. The project works with the state cooperative extension service in designing curricula, training, and networking of resources. The success of this project stemmed from the care with which the project staff members worked with an advisory group on a county-by-county basis and trained local residents to teach the classes. With limited resources, community groups learned how to adapt educational strategies to their rural problems and to identify ways technology can spur economic development.

Both of these models involve participatory research, an integrated approach that combines research, education, and action on issues considered important to a community. Central to this approach is the conviction that residents of a community can learn to define their issues, do most of their own research, educate one another, and participate in collective activities to solve their problems. When higher education works with community groups in this process and assists in providing the tools to identify and analyze the varied resources a community has, a new learning constituency is established. This permits communities to look at how large economic forces affect them, to identify the possible options for affecting the local economy, to decide on the most desirable approaches, and to develop the best possible strategies. This method calls for involving as many community citizens as possible throughout the process.

Higher education-business partnerships on behalf of the learners

Higher education-business partnerships have been around for quite sometime and the successes are evident. Benefits include the following: adult workers updating their employment skills to match job market demands, businesses keeping a skilled work force, and college enrolling a continuous flow of students.

The impetus for higher education to get involved in economic development is usually an immediate and specific need arising from rapid changes in labor market conditions. This urgency encourages employers, faculty members, and advisors to operate at first thinking only in the short term. Conversely, in today's technological world of work, employers are also providing evidence that job training is not enough. The education policy director for the American Enterprise Institute, Dennis Doyle, states,

> Businesses need employees who are problem solvers, self-starters who can think critically and independently. They are not looking for narrowly trained workers.

The idea of higher education having some kind of role in the economic concerns of the country is not new, and whether a college or university is just gearing up for a connection to economic development or is already involved, another question should be considered: beyond immediate job skills, what are the real educational benefits to the adult learners?

Higher education's links to economic development or partnerships with businesses could be a window of opportunity for learners to plug into a new kind of liberal education. It is probably useful to distinguish between the *liberal arts,* traditionally defined as a substantive body of knowledge defining and shaping culture, society, and ideas, and *liberal education,* a learning experience liberating one personally and providing the skills and knowledge to be more effective, self-confident, competent and self-directed. Instead of conducting only short-term planning, effective community economic development could use the linkages and partnerships as vehicles to help adult learners develop the fundamental knowledge and skills necessary to know how to *continue* to learn in their expanding economic society. The right balance of occupational, academic, and critical thinking skills could build the foundation necessary for learners to keep from being locked out of jobs and to be more responsible consumers, citizens, and family members. This, of course, presupposes that higher education can retool and gear career counseling, training, and liberal education to adults in the context of their local labor markets.

An educational strategy including a perception and language that emphasize community needs could help point the way toward long-term, effective community economic development that brings people together to meet the needs of all in the work place. The natural human desire for community interdependence can be a powerful force in countering an economic direction that trends to value corporate profit above people, families, and neighborhoods.

One scenario could include community efforts to create an effective balance between the skills of current occupations and the skills of knowing how to anticipate and plan for changes on an individual, industry, and community basis. Higher education could learn along with communities and help provide adult learners with the tools for foreseeing how to make decisions about necessary job changes, further education and training, and the implications for their lifestyles. Informed participation by local communities in decisions about their economic development recognizes the power of the people in truly democratic decision making.

Institutional Policies and Economic Development Programs

13

Universities, Centers, and Economic Development: Converting Rhetoric to Reality

Marshall Kaplan

The author is dean of the Graduate School of Public Affairs at the University of Colorado at Denver.

Many public university presidents and chancellors have become enamored with the role of their university in guiding their state's and/or community's proper economic development. Their speeches, whether before regents, students, or legislators, frequently call attention to the ostensible linkages between their educational institutions and facilities and local jobs, income and prosperity. Indeed, if measured by rhetoric, campuses' roles as economic multipliers and/or as strategic economic variables in the competition for defense contracts, high technology, and employment often appear to have supplanted their role as educational institutions.

To some extent, the conversion of presidents, chancellors, and even some deans to supply-side economics is understandable. While the idea may not sell easily in the halls of ivy, it does sell rather well in the halls of state and local government capitols and in the board rooms of many affluent corporations. Even if the relationships are tenuous or little understood, a college's public image of importance to its region's economimc health or revitalization may well be a ticket to survival and to resources.

Implicit if not explicit in the new popularity granted the public university's ostensible role in state and local economic development is the university's assumed willingness to *play* a role. Again and again one hears, "The university can help the state define economic possibilities," "the university can provide the skills and ideas necessary to generate investment," "the university can help foster public-private collaboration," "the university can become a partner in the state's, area's, and community's healthy economic growth."

The new economic agenda, if not always precise, is at least expansive. It optimistically suggests that universities will increasingly foster faculty and student involvement in various applied efforts related to research, training, technical assistance, mediation, and facilitation. It fosters the feeling that outreach finally will be perceived as an extension of the classroom and the laboratory, that theory and practice, model building and experience will be but two sides of the same educational coin. It offers hope that education will be less hide-bound and that "bundling-board" attitudes, often separating town and gown, will be declared off limits.

To those of you who, like me, have argued that this nation's public universities, particularly urban universities, must restructure and reform their academic programs and behavior patterns to survive and flourish, changes suggested by the university's newly found economic agenda should be welcome. But converting what may be a short-term fad to a long-term window of opportunity will require more than applause. It will require an understanding of the conventional university behavior patterns that stand in the way of institutionalizing academic outreach activities as a valued and, indeed, necessary part of academic programs.

In this context, our collective experience as educators is not good—perhaps for some justifiable reasons. Concern about the quality of professional education has not led to solid internal or external evaluations of the core curriculum and/or its relationship to the arts and humanities; concern about the lack of prestige granted applied research has not led to a willingness to critique (and set) the standards governing its implementation; concern about the minimal willingness of universities to grant credibility to training and technical assistance efforts has not been matched by equal concern for linkages between both and the raison d'etre of universities: educating students. We have sometimes been our own worst enemies. Or as Pogo says, "We have met the enemy, and he is us."

In this context, I would like to mention lessons learned from my own experiences, the experiences of my faculty colleagues, and our recent efforts to help other universities link outreach to academic program efforts.[1] Although we have not by any means developed a modern-day paradigm of professional education and/or its relationship to outreach activities in economic development, we have developed some approaches to both that have won acclaim.[2] They offer insight into the development of effective, evolving linkages between academic programs and applied research, technical assistance, training and mediation, and particularly into a university's role in economic development.

A center for public-private sector cooperation

Four years ago, when I became dean of the Graduate School of Public Affairs (GSPA) at the University of Colorado at Denver, GSPA established two new centers: the Center for the Improvement of Public Management and the Center for Public-Private Sector Cooperation. Both centers were initially funded with a $1,000,000 grant from the Piton and Gates Foundations. Both centers, as their names suggest, focused on building the state's capacity to govern and provide its residents with expanded quality-of-life choices. Both centers, in their agendas, granted primacy and visiblity to important activities intended to permit the university to help state and local government, public and private sectors respond to economic development objectives. Following are illustrations of center activities.

■ *Facilitation-Mediation*. The centers provide research support and mediation/facilitation efforts for several major public-private sector colaborative projects. In one case, the centers receive credit for generating a successful, multimiliondollar, public-private sector partnership involving a housing-driven, school-desegregation, new town-in-town development; in another, the centers helped two competing jurisdictions and a private developer resolve a conflict over a large regional shopping center and forge an agreement on tax-base sharing and sharing costs for key metro services.

■ *Applied Research*. The centers have initiated several crucial studies important to the state's economic development. They have staffed and advised the Governor's Public-Private Sector Housing Needs Task Force, the Legislative Capital Needs Committee, and the Governor's Metro Forum. At the request of the state, they have completed strategic studies on high-technology development; at the request of the Commission on the Arts and Humanities, they have analyzed of the economic impact of arts and culture on Colorado; at the request of a Colorado county, they have studied welfare diversion.

■ *Training*. The centers administer several different training programs for both the public and private sector. Training modules include such subjects as economic development strategies, public-private sector collaboration, leadership and economic development.

■ *Technical Assistance.* The centers provide technical assistance to state agencies, local governments, and the private sector. They have helped several communities initiate public-private sector investment strategies, helped the state Private Industry Councils (PICs) develop appropriate training and employment strategies, and worked on public-private sector capital-investment options.

The centers have become, in a relatively short time, highly visible, positively perceived institutions within the state. According to many outside reviews of center activities, they have had a significant and unique impact on the area's quality of life and on the choices open to its residents.

The centers have also played a major strategic role in the development of GSPA as a solid recognized academic entity and CU-Denver as a respected urban university. Their agendas have increased faculty reserach and publications. The centers have helped faculty members convert textbook knowledge to real-world applications and have increased public-private sector acceptance of the university's relevance to the community.

Lessons learned

Despite increasing acknowledgment by universities that their applied roles are varied and important to survival and growth; despite increasing recognition by universities that their applied roles, if structured appropriately, are important to their primary educational mission, centers have not and will not find life easy within them. Centers, if they are doing their job, will be taking risks in institutions where risk taking perhaps legitimately is sometimes questioned. Centers, if they are doing their job, will be pushing boundaries of outreach definitions in institutions where outreach is sometimes viewed in pejorative terms. Centers, if they are doing their job, will be testing the definitions of academic relevance and will be challenging conventional academic ground rules in institutions where stable and predictable definitions of both are viewed as essential.

Creative tension between centers and universities has and will continue to help both mature. To ensure that tension is creative and not debilitating will require us to draw from successful experience. Following are some critical lessons from my own involvement, and from the experiences of universities with which we are working.

Lesson 1—Secure an appropriate institutional home in the university. Absolute wisdom concerning where centers like our own should be placed within a university is absent. But based on experience at UCD and our work with other universities, I would place my bet on a "live" dean in an involved or public-policy-relevant school. Locations in or with a vice chancellor for academic affairs and/or a graduate school may look good on paper but generally do not work. Despite the best of intentions, the centers quickly tilt toward or are imaged by the "academic" and equally as quickly risk losing private- or public-sector support or interest. Rather than serve as a bridge between town and gown, between theory and practice, centers located in a wholly academic environment generally end up administering a rather narrowly defined, wholly academic work program.

There are other reasons for situating centers involved in economic development directly in schools, particularly professional schools, or schools related to public- or public-private sector policy issues. Clearly, deans and colleagues of such schools have a vested "academic interest" in promoting roles of such centers and in seeking funding for them. They are important to the relevance of schools of public affairs, business, planning, etc. They are often crucial to strategies for expanding faculty and classroom experiences. They are necessary to extend student internships and job opportunities. They play an important role in securing visibility and necessary external relationships.

Lesson II—Put and keep your academic house in order. The economic development roles of centers and universities are still nonconventional. Their visibility as well as their immersion in "applied" agendas threaten many traditionalists. Both run counter to academic behavior patterns, and both, if successful in paying off for the university, suggest consideration of amended academic behavior patterns. Although universities, of all places, should tolerate, indeed welcome, "a thousand flowers," tolerance in an academic environment is frequently academic.

Centers and/or the types of programs they run can and will be critiqued and their life legitimately threatened if they are seen as a diversion and/or if their administrative and academic shelter is not built on tough bedrock. If the schools that operate or are responsible for centers are weak or perceived as weak, they will be subject to flak directed in part toward the development and evoluton of their centers. The schools' program becomes a surrogate for and often must absorb the criticisms of the centers.

Attention to efforts to reform, strengthen, and enhance academic programs is a legitimate and necessary center development strategy. Both should/ must proceed hand in hand. In our own case, GSPA's visible and purposeful progress as an academic division played a crucial role in focusing internal dialogue on where it should be: the role and mission of the centers and the importance of the centers to GSPA and UCD.

Lesson III—Drive your outreach program by your academic program and not vice versa. Remember what business we are in. Our first and primary role is the proper education of our students. A center's appropriateness should ultimately be justified by its effect on a school's academic growth and on the related choices it offers faculty members and students.

Centers—no matter how successful community activities or economic development ojectives—would justifiably incur university criticsm and termination if they were not ultimately related in a symbolic and substantive manner to the growth and enhancement of GSPA's academic program. The centers would be out on the literal limb if they were not part of GSPA's strategy to secure top academic ranking.

Lesson IV—Define your initial agenda wisely. Centers, no matter how carefully nurtured, are vulnerable, particularly until they have become an accepted part of the university. A focus on economic development and/or strategic options to achieve the same will make them even more vulnerable. The subjects involved are often politically risky. Research, when it occurs, generally relies on secondary data and evolving methodological techniques. Training and technical assistance relies more on interdisciplinary backgrounds than on single-discipline knowledge. Causal linkages between efforts and success or failure, benefits and costs, are often difficult to discern immediately and clearly.

From scholars and/or scholar practitioners one will get four or more opinions on the correct way to set or secure an agenda or work program. To some extent, young centers are subject to demand-supply equations. "Go with the market" is not a bad strategy as long as sufficient room is left to define strategic areas of opportunity and as long as the ultimate objective is to match agenda to capacity.

At the outset, GSPA's centers, apart from responding to requests for assistance from the public and private sector, purposely decided to initiate a number of high-risk, potentially high-impact, economic-development-related projects. Our decision was premised on the felt need to build quickly a constituency among Denver's and the state's public and private leadership for UCD, GSPA, and the centers. Our failure to do so, we believed, would only strengthen the image problems faced by the university; would cater to those in the community who doubted that academics could and would play relevant policy roles; and would weaken our ability within the university to control our own fate. We had secured $1,000,000 on the bet that we could do things differently—that we could help make the university a useful partner in the state's and city's development. Center staff members felt the need to prove themselves quickly and to create the type of outside support that, because of center success, would "go to bat" for the centers internal and external to the university.

Lesson V—Hire staff in a strategic manner. No one wants to hire staff membes who are inappropriate. However, defining appropriate is often difficult and made more so by resource constraints and often bizarre university hiring practices.

Our success in establishing the centers' reputation both in and outside the university resulted largely from our luck and, I hope, wisdom in paying attention to staffing objectives. In this context, somewhat contrary to usual university practice regarding centers, in order to collapse the time it would take to build the confidence of Denver's public- and private-sector leadership, we purposely sought and secured center leaders whose state and local reputations as doers matched their reputations as thinkers. Initially, at least, we did not want the centers to be perceived as merely a think tank or as ivory tower academics. We wanted to present ourselves as individuals who could marry solid ideas about economic development to equally solid action. The center's first hirees were chosen as much for their political skills as for their mental acumen.

Only subsequently to hiring the center leaders did we go after the best possible research staff. Our obvious hope, at this juncture, was to generate creditable "paper" analyses, to respond continually well to "where's the beef"-type questions. Luckily, the length of time it took to hire a balanced staff in place was relatively brief. Colorado's mountains and amenity package helped us create attractive surrogates for higher salary remuneration available elsewhere.

Lesson VI—Develop academic and institutional credibility. Centers at most universities find it easy to gain applause and difficult to secure respect. Ours are no different. Despite the centers' ability to "win friends and influence people" on behalf of the university, despite the centers' real impact on the state's and community's economic development efforts, despite the center's tangible, positive effect on GSPA's academic program, despite the centers' own significant research and publication record, they have sometimes found life difficult in the university.

Lesson VII—Protect your backside against risk. As noted earlier, the centers, particularly those involved in economic development, should, must, will be taking on numerouse risky agenda items. Indeed, given the fact that most urban communities are resource constrained, almost by definition, most of the policy-defining activities of centers will be politically fragile.

To avoid risk taking would condemn centers to irrelevance or worse (lack of outside support), yet to avoid initiating steps to minimize exposure is irresponsible. Our own "learn-by-experience" ground rules include:

1. Try to secure requests for center involvement from all significantly affected public- and private-sector parties before agreeing to involvement,

2. Try to secure small amounts of support funds from many people rather than large amounts, from a few people—in other words, avoid the image of being bought or becoming a perceived advocate of one party or another to public-policy disputes,

3. Use formal or informal advisory boards of public-private sector leaders and/or scholars, when possible and relevant, to review and comment on center efforts,

4. On projects likely to go public, define an honest and sustained informal relationship with the media.

Lesson VIII—Create appropriate faculty incentives. Sustained faculty involvement in the centers is essential if we are to meet the new and complex economic development roles assigned us by our leaders. It is also essential if centers are to find a stable niche within our universities and if our universities' and schools' academic programs are to be enriched by centers.

To secure extended faculty involvement has not and will not be easy. Although we have had some modest success, the pain has often been intense. Clearly, current university rules and behavior patterns dissuade faculty members from center participation. Achievement of closer linkages between faculty members and centers will require us to attend continuously to the following:

1. My university, like yours, articulates the need to grant community service and teaching recognition in addition to research and publication in promotion, tenure, and merit pay decisions. But my university, like yours, has trouble defining what weight to allocate to community service and teaching in such decisions (i.e., merit pay, promotion, and tenure). Clearly, if we are to gain across-the-board faculty involvement in the broad range of center activities— apart from research—we will have to find a way to acknowledge their validity in terms of faculty rewards.

2. My university, like yours, has extra compensation rules that, while legitimate, perhaps in their historical premises, need evaluation in current salary constraints. They inhibit or deny remuneration for work done on grants and so on within the university. In a perverse way—perverse in the context of center and university development objectives—they almost force faculty members to engage in outside consulting efforts. Work done outside the university may be reimbursed if it occupies no more than a certain percentage of a faculty member's time. Yet the same work done within the university often secures only intrinsic rewards or possible rewards during promotion, tenure, and remuneration reviews. Faculty members are asked to choose between *possible* academic salvation if they bring supported projects into the university and *probable* remuneration if they stay outside the university. Generally, the choice is not a tough one to make for many who have tight budgets and mouths to feed.

3. My university, like yours, has placed more of a premium on basic than applied research. Indeed, we, like you, often engage in endless arguments about the wisdom of both and their contributions to the university.

My own views, while certainly debatable, are clear. Tax-supported, urban public universities have an obligation to engage in and encourage applied research. Questions on impact, product quality, and process ground rules are legitimate and need to be examined. But to continue the argument over the relevance of applied vs. basic or basic vs. applied research is silly. Boundaries rarely are clear. Incentives must be constructed that grant equality or near equality to both.

Lesson IX—Avoid the myth of coordination; choose the benefits of process and collegiality. Coordination in the abstract in a bureaucracy is often the kiss of death. Note that institutions are rarely asked to coordinate or to share responsibilities until they are successful.

A good friend of mine, now a U.S. Senator, and a former academic, once told me that "coordination, unless strategically defined and bounded, is sometimes the hobgoblin of foolish minds." He meant that we spend so much time coordinating that very little occurs of value and/or that coordinated decisions are often lowest-common-denominator decisions. The less confident a university is, the more concern it has about coordination by regulation and fiat.[3]

Center leadership and leadership responsibilities should be clear. Responsibility should be granted and should be precisely defined if centers are to be successful. Shared leadership between more than one person or one school spells disaster.

This is not to say that centers do not have a real and sustained responsibility to the schools they are in and, in turn, to their institutions: clearly, they do. Their agendas, being politically and substantively complex, require a special obligation to the university hierarchy to inform, review, compromise, and indeed consider alternative strategies before rather than after the fact.

Similarly, center successes, whether of the fund-raising or substantive variety, require deans and/or center directors to build relationships with other schools and to share opportunities. This makes good political and common sense.

But imposing structure or regulations to achieve coordination is neither in the university's or a center's best interests. Responsible professionals governed by professional ground rules should be able to substitutue collegiality and process for structure and regulation.

Lesson X—Build a secure, balanced financial base. Academic (read *center*) freedom and choices are often tested when academic budgets are minimal. Earlier, it was indicated how important it is to secure broad-based center support in order to minimize political risk. Broad-based financial support is essential for intellectual survival.[4]

To secure continuous private-sector and foundation help will require visible university contributions. In our case, outside contributors justifiably indicate, "We are willing to help. . . . You are doing wonderful things. . . . You are helping the community and the university . . . but our continued support is dependent on the university's willingness to really come to the table."

University economics often make center support difficult. But to the extent deans and center leaders can convince university leaders that centers are important to the university role and mission and to its quest for academic excellence, the odds of success increase. There is cause for optimism if only because centers have a tremendous ability to leverage marginal university resources. The increased public commitments of universities to cooperate with their respective communities in economic development should help centers and/or related programs win a fairer share of resources.

Lessons drawn from experience are primarily valuable if they fit new and/or changing situations. As Leonardo Da Vinci said, "Experience does not err; only . . . judgments err by expecting from her what is not in her power." We must be careful not to look at the future by casting in cement the problems (and solutions) of the past. But the "winds of change are blowing." Public universities, perhaps because of economic circumstance and perhaps because of our own willingness to indicate we are less than what we could be, will be vastly different institutions in the near future. If, drawing on the wisdom borne of past successes and failures, we can help our institutions enrich their academic role and mission by helping them understand, define, and play out important economic development roles, we will have made a real contribution.

Notes

[1] The Aetna Foundation has provided the University of Colorado with a small grant to help other universities replicate our experiences.

[2] from Harvard University, foundations, local media, and the accrediation team.

[3] There are alternate and acceptable models of coordination. Information sharing, peer group communication, etc. are, in spirit, more relevant to universities. But sometimes spirit doesn't catch up with practice.

[4] University overhead and billing rules make it difficult for centers to break even. This fact should increase university willingness to assist centers. It is at least a legitimate and necessary argument at budget-making time.

14

Establishing an Effective, University-Based Technical Assistance Program

Karl Turner

The author is chairman of Business Administration and Economics at Xavier University of Louisiana.

The entrepreneur confronts a host of technical, financial, and managerial problems in moving from idea to prototype of production and distribution. During the early stages of development, new entrepreneurial ventures are often undercapitalized and understaffed. During the preoperational stages of business development, the entrepreneur often operates on a compelling and, in some cases, blind drive to succeed. This drive is frequently not supported by a detailed or polished business plan, or an in-depth marketing study that can serve as the basis for developing a marketing strategy. In fact, one 1983 study entitled *Survey of Minority Business in New Orleans,* conducted by the Xavier Economic Development Center, revealed that in the vast majority of new and old minority-owned ventures: (1)sales volumes will not yield internal funds for growth; (2) the asset base is less than adequate; (3) access to external funds for growth is limited; (4) managers often have little formal business training and few connections inside the systems of the public and private sectors that will facilitate the successful marketing of their products.[1]

Developing a sophisticated business plan, investing time and resources in a marketing study, and obtaining the necessary first- and second-tier financing can require costly investments in consulting services. The same constraints and lack of high-caliber professional consulting services hold true for existing firms that experience financial, technological, or managerial difficulties. Access to capital and technical assistance is prerequisite to profitability for any new venture or any existing small business.

More and more often, business owners and managers turn to universities for management and technical assistance. This trend has created an entirely new role for educational institutions. Policy makers now want and expect to derive economic benefits from government-funded university research and from the pool of talent available at public and private educational institutions. Businesses respond by sponsoring more research and relying more heavily on colleges and universities to meet their training and management assistance needs. Thus, the historic chasm and adversarial relationship between academic and entrepreneurial "cultures" is giving way to a search for collaboration and cooperation.

Partnership profiles

There historically has been a perception that the pool of management and technological expertise at public and private colleges and universities has been underutilized. Until recently, few universities have embraced information and technology transfer as a university research responsibility. Tenure and publication requirements have reinforced the bias against technical outreach programs and applied research, while national laboratories and federal mission-directed research agencies have been viewed as vehicles to increase the flow of new scientific knowledge. Now that the knowledge-based resources on college campuses are viewed as essential elements in the new economic infrastructure, the question arises on how to develop programs to match business requirements with the knowledge-based resources available at universities. Industry looks to the nation's universities for talent, new ideas, and basic research facilities, whereas universities need the financial support and the technical know how that industry can provide. Based on the experiences of several universities that have developed effective technical assistance and business consulting programs, the key to success lies in anticipating potential problems and developing guidelines for averting them or addressing them as they occur.

A great deal depends on the resource base and leadership of the university. Regardless of the internal and external means by which universities have become engaged in economic development, most university-based technical assistance centers can be grouped under one or more of the following Business-Higher Education Partnership Profiles. Some examples are listed under each.

Human Resource Development
- Extended degrees, off campus education, continuing education, conferences
- Contract education: inhouse training
- Telecommunication: microwave, cable delivery systems
- Faculty-Industry exchange

Technology Transfer
- University of Wisconsin Office of Industrial Research and Technology Transfer
- Pennsylvania State University Technical Assistance Program (PENTAP)

Industrial Extension Program
- Iowa State University of Science and Technology
- University of Arkansas Industrial Research and Extension Center
- Cooperatives

University-Based Research Centers
- Center for Integrated Systems: Stanford University
  —built partially by industrial funds
  —by 1982, center had seventeen sponsors and guaranteed commitments of $20 million for facilities; $8 million in defense contracts
  —Stanford owns patents, but results go to participating industries through favored licensing arrangements.
- Center for Welding Research, Ohio State University
- Center for Interactive Computer Graphics, Rensselaer Polytechnic Institute
- Center for Research on Polymers, University of Massachusetts
- Center for Energy Utilization Lab, Iowa State University

Research Collectives and Industrial Parks
Usually involve long-term, broad-based contracts involving a collection of universities and/or an entire sector of industries. Such research collectives and industrial parks tend to involve several universities in supporting research for an entire industry for the express purpose of increasing pure research and increasing the supply of professionals.
- Rensselaer Technology Park-Rensselaer Polytechnic Institute
- Central Florida Research Park-University of Central Florida
- Triangle University for Advanced Studies
- Ben Franklin Partnership
- Georgia Institute of Technology
- Stanford Research Park-Stanford University

- University of Alabama at Tuscaloosa Small Business Development Center
- Xavier University of Louisiana EDA University Center Program
- University of Wisconsin at Eau Claire Small Business Institute Program
- Advanced Technology Development Center, Georgia Tech

Joint Ventures: Business
- University of California at Stanford entered a joint arrangement with Engenics Inc., a bioengineering firm, to form a nonprofit Center for Biotechnolgy Research as a buffer between Engenics and the university to support university research and to make research available for creation of new business in genetic technology. The university gets exclusive patent rights; sponsoring corporations get exclusive sublicenses to exploit patents and discoveries.
- University Ventures Incorporated (UVI), University of Rochester. UVI was formed as a subsidiary to the University of Rochester and controls $68 million of $491 million in endowments.

Planning an effective program

All the above programs require administrators to consider policy issues: Should the university commit resources to economic development? If so, how much? What type of program? What are the potential outcomes for the university and the community? What are the legal ramifications of various consulting arrangements?

The university should articulate a policy statement that reflects its short- and long-term strategic goals for the program. All university-based technical assistance programs have at least two primary goals: to provide private-sector access to the pool of managerial and technical talent available on campus, and to provide an opportunity for faculty members and students to experience real-world conditions. Several factors should be evaluated early in order to avoid pitfalls and to formulate a strategic university policy clearly supportive of greater university-business partnerships. Depending on the leadership, the university may need to abandon historical preconceptions that restrict the role and intensity of involvement. Institutional policies and guidelines on such matters as tenure, teaching load, and publication requirements may need overhauling if such guidelines discourage outreach programs by professors and departments. Other questions for consideration by the university planning team include:
- What is the mission of the university?
- How does a particular economic development program assist the university in fulfilling its short- and long-term goals?
- What are the strengths of the university?
- What are the implications of targeting a specific type and size of business to serve?
- Aside from human resources, how much money is the university able and willing to dedicate to the program?
- How does the program complement or conflict with other existing private, state, or federally funded programs in the region?
- Should the economic development program in a specific college (i.e., business or engineering, etc.) or be made partially or totally autonomous?

The planning team should include the president and/or vice president, and possibly the planning and public relations directors. Long-term planning for the university-based technical assistance center should include an evaluation/support body such as a board or council whose primary function is strategic planning. This group should consist of university, business, and community representatives. Creating an advisory council is a proactive and strategic move by the university to establish direct contact with and support from local companies and financial institutions. The Xavier Economic Development Center has an eight-member advisory council of local civic leaders, entrepreneurs, representatives from the chamber of commerce, and university officials, including the executive vice president.

University officials must determine the type and organizational structure of the program. Will the program be a small business development center, an incubator, or part of the EDA-funded University Center Program? Will the program director report to the president, vice president, or chair of the department in which the program is housed? It is imperative that the program receive leadership and support from the president and or vice president. Without wholehearted support from top university officials, the program will flounder, and it will be impossible to build strong and lasting relationships with industry.

The program director must take a systematic approach to economic development planning and develp a plan of action to accomplish each project. Each party lays out what it expects the other party to do, what the end results will be, and, if applicable, the cost of services. As an example, during the 1984 Louisiana Exposition the Xavier EDC entered a memorandum of understanding with one vendor, Africa Unlimited, to provide management and accounting services. The scope of the agreement was narrow and served the interest of both parties. Faculty members and students were paid to study internal accounting controls, prepare the chart and book of accounts, and compile financial statements. The experience created a new direction and a new set of problems for the center. By using students and faculty and staff members from the center, it could provide limited accounting services, including a write-up service. But providing such services at below-market rates would in theory displace fledgling accounting service companies. Another issue concerns whether such fee-for-service arrangements subject the university to potential lawsuits that might arise from the center's failure to disclose errors, irregularities, and illegal acts, including possible fraud or defalcations.

Certainly there are benefits to students and faculty members from arrangements that enable them to use portable computers and integrated accounting programs to analyze real-world accounting problems. The risk can be minimized by structuring the financial service program to provide small business clients with short-term accounting and financial services. Accounting services should be limited to accounting systems review and design rather than prolonged services.

Ensuring continuity in staffing and program goals is crucial. To achieve any degree of credibility and sense of direction, university officials must provide the appropriate mix of monetary and nonmonetary incentives for the employees. Such incentives might include tuition-free enrollment in any class, travel opportunities, credit given to individuals responsible for the work and general integration of the staff into the organizational culture of the university.

Policy makers must be prepared to deal with negative results, which could include the following:

■ jealousy among professors participating in the program. The reverse of this situation is typically the case at smaller universities where faculty members are not motivated to participate because their excessive teaching load does not permit time to devote to the program. In such situations, the university must be prepared to provide release time as a motivation for participation. Paying part-time faculty members to teach courses while giving full-time faculty members release time devote to the technical assistance program will prove beneficial in the long run because such involvement can enable the institution to develop new alliances with industry and government, expand the university's resource base, attract more students, provide better education, and develop stimulating and useful research opportunities.

■ overburdened students who may not be able to maintain a high degree of professional responsibility to the business client while also keeping up with assignments in other courses

■ widely varying student skills

■ problems assessing the impact of consulting because the contract may end after a short time or because there is no systematic contact after completion of the project.

The program director and staff and faculty members involved should never be allowed to exploit the resources of the program. In the past, faculty members consulted with outside firms, but few started their own management consulting or accounting firm. When a faculty member owns a percentage of an outside company that is a client of the university center, some gauge is needed to determine when that percentage is high enough to present a conflict of interest. To allow faculty members or the center director to lease or use space for private business would confuse colleagues, support staff members, and students in determining whether a given project is part of an institutional responsibility or a private business activity.

State and federal policy makers should support the creation or expansion of university centers for business development. The SBA-funded Small Business Development Centers (SBDC), the Small Business Institute (SBI), and the University Center Program, funded by EDA, are three extremely important examples of the positive effects of the federal state role in facilitating university-based business consulting programs. SBDC goals and those of the SBI program are basically the same: to provide business consulting services through a cooperative arrangement between the federal government and a statewide network set up within a university system. According to *Business-Higher Education Development Strategies,* published in 1985 by the Northeast-Midwest Institute, Illinois is the only state to designate a state agency—the Department of Commerce and Community Affairs (DCCA)—as the lead SBDC organization. The Illinois model links the resources of universities throughout the state with participating businesses, rather than just one business department in a university. The Illinois model would seem to have the advantage of depoliticizing the choice of the designated lead institution while integrating the SBDC network well into the state's development plans. Another advantage would be direct access to university and government resources. The 1985 appropriation for the SBDC program was $28 million, and the program operates in thirty-five states.[2]

The EDA-funded University Center Program is another program that provides federal support for a nationwide higher education network to provide technical and management services to business and industry. There are approximately fifty EDA university centers in thirty-two states. The 1985 appropriation was approximately $3 million. The philosophy and flexible structure of this program provide an ideal structure to start a university-based technical assistance center. Rather than requiring the university to concentrate on small business development, EDA university centers permit universities to structure an outreach mission adapted to the economic development needs of their locales. Some concentrate entirely on support of economic development in urban areas; some emphasize economic development in rural areas; some emphasize rural economic development planning; still others provide technical assistance in such areas as robotics and technology transfer.

Because the university center program does not have the same stringent, nonfederal matching-fund requirements of the SBDC, it is of special importance to the historically black universities and other small colleges and universities interested in creating or expanding a university-based technical assistance program. The broad and flexible structure of the program permits schools with smaller resource bases to design a program innovative in nature and complementary to local and regional development philosophy and goals. Clearly, state and federal government agencies have a significant role in developing higher education networks to provide consulting services to business and industry. Considering its positive impact, the EDA university center program should be continued and expanded.

It is difficult to project the direction or outcome of a specific program. What begins as a simple faculty exchange program between a business and university may develop into a successful research or consulting arrangement. An extremely interesting and creative example is the not-for-profit joint venture project between the University System of New Hampshire and the Business and Industry Association of New Hampshire. These two groups formed a company called Venture Capital Network, Inc. The company's main purpose is to introduce venture capitalists to entrepreneurs.

It is important to both universities and businesses to influence economic development and to expand their own reputations. To accomplish this goal, each partner's resources must be exploited efficiently, and universities must be creative in developing new policies and procedures that reward faculty members and students for participating in technical assistance programs.

To be effective, university-based technical assistance centers must evolve out of a detailed understanding of the business and economic conditions within a commmunity and the strategic alternatives for business expansion and economic development.

Notes

[1]"Survey of Minority Business in New Orleans," Xavier Economic Development Center, Xavier University of Louisiana, 1984.

[2]P. Doyle and C. Brisson, "Business-Higher Education Development Strategies," Northeast-Midwest Institute, 1985.

15

Encouraging Faculty Involvement in University Economic Development Programs

Patricia Crosson

The author is associate professor of higher education at the University of Massachusetts-Amherst.

The case for an expanded role for higher education in local, regional, and national economic development rests on the recognition that knowledge—especially new discoveries and new applications—fuels economic development and that colleges and universities are enormous, publicly supported repositories of knowledge and talent. In this context, the major resource colleges and universities have to offer is the faculty—the producers and disseminators of knowledge. Faculty effort and activity is required if colleges and universities are to engage in economic development activities such as economic research and analysis, technical assistance, technology transfer, and human resource development. A crucial question for institutions, then, is how to generate faculty interest and involvement. How can colleges and universities encourage greater faculty involvement in economic development activities? How might that involvement be channeled so that the whole of faculty economic development activity can become greater than the sum of its parts—that is, so that faculty effort can be aggregated into an institutional response?

To answer these questions, colleges and universities need to address several complex and interrelated issues, including reward and incentive systems; workload; consulting and salary policies; and larger questions of institutional values, infrastructures, and faculty morale. There are no easy answers. Also, it is important to recognize that there is no single strategy that will work for all, or even most, colleges and universities. Diverse traditions, missions, purposes, constituencies, and external relationships require different approaches and strategies. However, there are some approaches that might prove useful to colleges and universities struggling with the "how" questions.

Workload

For many good reasons, neither society nor the higher education community have been terribly precise about what they expect faculty members to do. Faculty roles are usually stated in rather broad terms—teaching, research and scholarly activity, institutional service, and public service. The specific activities in each area and the particular mix of activities will vary with institutional type and with the particular characteristics of the discipline or professional field. Consistent with the image of a faculty member as a semiautonomous professional, institutions expect adequate performance in the agreed-upon areas rather than a mandated number of working hours. An exception is in the area of teaching and advising, for which colleges and universities often require a specific number of hours each week.

Studies of faculty workload have been plagued by such methodological problems as reliance on self-reports and lack of longitudinal data, but

> hundreds of studies over many years yield convergent data indicating that faculty members report that they devote an average of 55 hours per week during the academic year to professional activities. Studies based on methods other than faculty reports indicate an average of 45 hours per week. (The most significant differences, however, are individual differences. . . . Some faculty work fewer than 30 hours a week while others work more than 70.[1]

The general terms used to define faculty work and institutional expectations and the imprecision with which their work accomplishments are calculated and measured make it difficult to get a handle on issues of faculty workload. Yet it is important to do so because the automatic reaction from most faculty members to any requests from their colleges and universities for increased activity in the area of regional, local, or national economic development will be that workloads, expectations, and pressures are already too heavy. At present, there is considerable pressure in higher education for more and/or better work in each of the faculty responsibility areas—for better teaching and greater attention to undergraduate education, for improvement in the quality of graduate programs, for greater involvement in service activities at institutional and extrainstitutional levels, and above all, for improvements in research and scholarship in order to enhance the institution's reputation for quality.

Workload pressures are particulaly intense in the areas that colleges and universities rely on most heavily for economic development activities—namely, business, engineering, and computer sciences. These fields are under the heaviest enrollment pressures at present and are having difficulty keeping faculty positions filled.

Bowen and Schuster argue that, given already-high workloads and limited amounts of time, pressure to do more of one type of activity will force the faculty simply to replace another activity. Most faculty members allocate time and effort among their many responsibilities to end up with what they consider a tolerable total workload.[2] They may resist and resent pressure to change their allocations if they feel they do not have adequate time to fulfill a certain area responsibly. They also resist extensive or long-term, upward adjustments to the total workload expectations.

Therefore, colleges and universities asking their faculty for greater involvement in economic development activities, whatever they may be, should be willing to have other activity displaced and ideally should be willing to tell the faculty what areas can be dropped. They should be willing to state clearly the kinds of activity that are highly valued and endorsed. They must guard against the "everything is most important in our institution" phenomenon.

It is difficult to imagine that colleges and universities will be seriously willing to do this, however. Commitments to economic development activities are much more likely to be added to the already long and growing list of desirable public-service activities to which academe pays lip service but which everyone on the inside knows occupy a distant third place in the hierarchy of institutional values. Internal values and reward systems will emphasize research and scholarly activity; financial pressures and changing demographics will increase the number of students in instruction and advising and/or the amount of effort required for underprepared students. Public service will remain that third mission we wish we had time for but don't.

In a forthcoming book on universities and the knowledge needs of society, Ernest Lynton and Sandra Elman argue persuasively that higher education needs a fundamental change in values to accord importance and worth to a much broader spectrum of faculty professional activity. Lynton and Elman would add synthesis, interpretation, application, and broad dissemination of knowledge to the currently valued pursuits of basic research, scholarly and creative activity, and traditional campus-based teaching. They argue that such additions would not only strengthen the contributions and connections with external groups but enhance basic research and teaching. If colleges and universities take these suggestions seriously, faculty members would gain needed institutional moral support for involvement in economic development activities.[3]

Such a shift or broadening of basic institutional values would allow colleges and universities to accommodate many important economic development activities (e.g., economic research and analysis, technical assistance, new product development) as research and scholarly work and thus relate a number of human resource development activities (e.g., on-site training and retraining programs, special seminars and workshops) to teaching.

Conceptual adjustment will not solve all the problems. The pressures for "more and better" in all areas of faculty activity will continue, but changing the perspective allows institutions to include a wider variety of economic development activities within normal faculty workload expectations.

Reward systems

Most academic administrators and faculty members believe that rewards and incentives are the critical factors in institutional efforts to increase faculty involvement in economic development activities. The basic assumptions are Skinnerian—activity rewarded will continue to be performed while activity unrewarded will be dropped.

There is some evidence to support this assumption. In a review of faculty research performance that considered a variety of explanations for successful, productive research on the part of faculty members—including psychological explanations (ability and motivation), theories of cumulative advantage, and disciplinary norms and reinforcement—Cresswell concluded that "of all the explanations for research performance, reinforcement may be the most important because of the strong positive relationship between its measures and high performance levels."[4] The most positive reinforcers for research performance were those associated with publication (e.g., citation, early publication, rate of publication), but promotion was also important. When faculty members who had worked the same number of years in higher education were examined, "those with a higher rank tended to be higher research producers than those with a lower rank."[5] The problem, of course, is to determine which is cause and which effect. Does rank cause high productivity or vice versa? Interestingly, tenure appears to exercise little influence on research productivity. Holley, Neumann, and Blackburn, Behymer, and Hall all note stable or decreased research productivity after the award of tenure.[6]

For public service, the presumed link between rewards and activity levels is not clear. Most faculty members believe that public service activities are not rewarded, and many would argue that as institutions have paid increasing attention to research and scholarship over the past decade, levels of public service have decreased. Institutional reports and various surveys, however, testify to extensive amounts of public-service activity in colleges and universities.[7] There are no mechanisms for measuring the amount of public service in higher education, no longitudinal studies of service activity, and no empirical studies linking reward systems and public service; consequently, evidence is lacking to support or refute faculty opinion. Because faculty economic development activities are likely to fall under the general rubric of public service or professional activity in most colleges and universities, the lack of clear-cut evidence on the relationship between academic rewards and the amount of public-service activity is particulary troublesome. For the purposes of this discussion, however, it is assumed the relationship is strong and direct.

The most important rewards in higher education are tenure, promotion, salary, and merit increases. Other resources such as reduced teaching loads, graduate student support, secretarial assistance, sabbaticals, and funds for travel to conferences and other developmental purposes can be used as well. Important but intangible rewards include special honors and awards for meritorious service, which testify to recognition for valued contributions and confer esteem and respect. All of these rewards and incentives could be used by colleges and universities to encourage faculty involvement in applied research, technology transfer, technical assistance, and other economic development activities.

Tuckman's studies of reward structures in higher education suggest that the publication of articles and, to a lesser extent, books and other scholarly achievements are the most highly rewarded faculty activities in terms of salary and promotion. He notes important differences among institutions and among disciplines and professional fields, however, and acknowledges the difficulty of assessing rewards and activities that cannot be quantified.[8] There have been few other empirical attempts to examine the relationship between faculty activities and faculty rewards.

Over the years, colleges and universities have established elaborate policies and procedures to assess and judge faculty activity for purposes of personnel decisions and rewards. Are research and scholarly activity rewarded because of institutional value systems, or are they rewarded because it is somewhat easier to assess, measure, and quantify those activities than the less easily quantifiable service activities? It is impossible to know for certain. There is no doubt that at many colleges and universities, research and scholarly activities are highly valued. It is also true, however, that assessment measures for research and scholarship are more clearly elaborated. It is not easy to judge scholarly quality and potential, but faculty members recognize the necessity of making such judgments and are usually willing to do it. So, too, with teaching. Although teaching may or may not be highly valued by faculty members, it is commonly recognized as an essential activity. Mechanisms to evaluate the quality for teaching for purposes of basic personnel decisions have been developed and are widely used in higher education. In the area of public service, uncertainties about the worth and importance of such activities in higher education are compounded by inadequate assessment and evaluation mechanisms; i.e., even if we want to reward such activity, we often do not know how.

There has been extensive discussion of the necessary connection between reward systems and faculty service activities in the literature but few agreements and little progress. It would be foolish to attempt "ideal" or "model" reward structures to apply to all service activities at all types of colleges and universities. There are too many differences in institutional purposes and priorities and in appropriate forms and types of services. There are no simple prescriptions for how to count, assess, and evaluate service activities for purposes of reward. The same applies to economic development activities. The ideal blend of amount and types of activity, and the appropriate system for rewarding that activity, must be tailored to the specific circumstances and opportunities of each college and university.

It is feasible, however, to consider a reward system adapted to Lynton and Elman's broader conception of institutionally valued activity that includes synthesis, interpretation, and dissemination of knowledge. Lynton and Elman also argue for a reward system that recognizes professional activity:

> Without a substantial adaptation of the faculty reward system all efforts at greater university outreach will continue to be what they have been in the majority of institutions: well intended but largely ineffective rhetoric. It is not enough simply to say: this ought to happen. We need to address ourselves in a pragmatic and realistic way to how it can be made to happen. And in this the pivotal element is to find ways of assuring that the broader range of faculty professional activity is being taken as seriously as the more traditionaly scholarly engagements.[9]

In a specific and helpful monograph on professional service and faculty rewards prepared as part of a long-term project of the National Association of State Universities and Land-Grant Colleges Division of Urban Affairs, Sandra Elman and Sue Marx Smock offer some preliminary guidelines for a reward system for professional service. Their suggestions apply equally well to the somewhat narrower category of faculty economic development activities. Elman and Smock argue first that labels of teaching, research, or service ard irrelevant. To them, the professional work that should be rewarded in academic institutions includes activity that

- creates new knowledge
- trains others in the discipline or area of expertise
- aggregates and interprets knowledge to make it understandable and useful, or
- disseminates the knowledge to the appropriate user or audience.[10]

Further, they argue that reward systems for professional service work, as defined above, require the application of the same rigorous standards of evaluation applied to teaching and research—no more or less. They suggest that colleges and universities

- should decide on the categories of professional service that will be rewarded.

The monograph discusses the following categories in some detail: applied research, consultation and technical assistance, special forms of instruction (e.g., seminars, workshops) the development of new products, and clinical work and performance. With the exception of the last, these same categories might effectively encompass the range of faculty economic development activity and contributions to business and industry. Elman and Smock note, however, that it is important that institutions decide on the appropriate categories and inform their faculty about what kinds of activities the institution considers worthwhile.

■ should, as a matter of policy, "assign weights to the specific activities within professional service." so that faculty members will know which types of activities will be rewarded.[11] The weights, like the categories, will vary according to several factors, but institutions should let the faculty know, as far in advance as possible, the ratings that will be used. Applied research might be weighted most heavily for purposes of reward in one professional area, while in another the priority might be specialized training programs considered more responsive to external and faculty professional development needs. Obvioulsy, institutions cannot be expected to be too precise in the matter of weighting because many different kinds of activities might be equally important and because judgments must vary according to specific situations, but the principle of clear signals for the faculty is an important one.

■ should not merely count the amount of professional service activity but should also make judgments about its quality. Institutions should create "structural mechanisms for evaluating the level of quality . . . [that are] the same as, or at the very least, compatible with the mechanisms for evaluating teaching and research."[12]

One structural mechanism stressed by Elman and Smock is documentation. They suggest that colleges and universities develop guidelines for documentation to ensure that faculty members provide adequate information about the activity so that qualitative assessments can be made. The documentation required would correspond to the type of activity. For applied research activities, a report or summary describing the effort, its significance, and its results would be in order. For technical assistance and consulting activities, faculty members could be asked to provide full descriptions including professional contributions, the importance or impact of the activity, and its relationship to the professional development of the faculty member. Off-campus instructional activities can be documented with syllabi, reading lists, materials used, or bulletins in much the same way as on-campus, credit teaching is documented.[13]

Documentation could be required for all types of economic development activities. Faculty members could be asked to describe the activity, discuss its significance to local or regional economic development, describe the particular knowledge or expertise demonstrated, describe the potential beneficiaries, and so forth. Smaller colleges might develop a single set of documentation guidelines; larger institutions might decentralize this requirement and ask each school or college to develop appropriate suggestions.

Another structural mechanism suggested by Elman and Smock is the use of appropriate external assessments of quality. Faculty committees and academic administrators can gather evidence of the quality of the professional service activity in much the same way that evidence is gathered of the quality of scholarship from faculty peers. Elman and Smock suggest asking professional association representatives, contractors, sponsors, participants, and other professionals, as appropriate to the specific activity, to provide assessments of quality and impact.[14]

For economic development activities, special teams of experts might be used to aid assessing quality and contribution. A committee of professional visitors for the college as a whole, or for each college or school, could be established to review faculty documents and prepare a qualitative assessment for the use of faculty personnel committees. The committees would review such assessments and prepare their own recommendations for tenure, promotions, or salary increases.

Beyond the adaptation of definitional, structural, and procedural aspects of reward systems to recognize faculty economic development activities, colleges and universities should search for creative approaches to use with tenured faculty members. The tenured faculty is the major resource and the most difficult to influence. Tuckman, speculating on the implications for academic reward systems of such present and future restraints as tight job markets, reduced resources, and an aging faculty, noted,

> Perhaps the more distressing aspect of our inquiry is the observation that the reward structure primarily favors performance when faculty have a large number of years left at work. In the absence of a change in the existing reward structure, it seems likely that as faculty members age, their incentive to remain productive will diminish. . . . What is needed is a reward structure that recognizes the need for incentives at the associate and full professor levels.[15]

Tuckman suggests increasing the number of academic ranks to provide more opportunities for promotion and salary advancement. He argues that the compression of salaries is increasingly discouraging to productivity in the later years. Colleges and universities might consider creating special titles and salaries for distinguished contributions to economic development activities, positions analogous to distinguished or chaired professorships.

Colleges and universities might also consider tying other incentives directly to commitment to economic development activities. For example, graduate student assistants, sabbatical leaves, travel funds, and secretarial assistance could all be used as inducements. A special "economic development activities" fund could be established, and faculty members could request money for specific projects. Such mechanisms already exist in most colleges and universities to support the research activities of young scholars and to encourage efforts to improve teaching.

The intangibles are also important. Colleges and universities could find ways to honor those faculty members participating in economic development programs that involve applied research, technical assistance, technology transfer, or dissemination. Professional associations and discipline-based societies could play important roles in this effort. If these groups, along with colleges and universities, broadened their conception of valued professional activity, it would be easier for colleges and universities to adjust internal reward systems.

Faculty consulting

Much current activity relating colleges and universities to business and industry results from the activities of individual faculty members serving as paid consultants. The question of whether this practice enhances or inhibits institutional efforts to be responsive to economic development needs is important but difficult to answer. On one side, it can be argued that colleges and universities most effectively respond by encouraging natural and direct linkages between faculty members and outside groups. It is also argued that allowing faculty members, particularly those in the high-demand areas such as business, engineering, and computer science, to supplement their salary encourages them to remain on campus and forgo more lucrative positions in business and industry. Furthermore, allowing faculty members to consult saves colleges and universities money and helps them avoid even greater disparities between salaries in low-demand and high-demand areas.

On the other side, paid consultants can be viewed as "double dipping." Faculty members are paid once by their institutions for public-service activities considered part of normal obligations and workload, and then again as consultants by government, business, and industry. Colleges and universities are criticized for trying to have it both ways—for taking credit for service activities actually paid for by others. It is further argued that such activities jeopardize the fulfillment of teaching and research obligations; engender numerous conflicts of interest for faculty members and their institutions; and create unfair competition in the market place when publicly subsidized faculty members compete with private consulting firms for interesting and lucrative projects.

The popular media paint a picture of jet set faculty entrepreneurs off in exotic places and presumably neglecting their students back home. We can all name faculty members whose earned income is many times their "full-time" salary. Yet the actual level of faculty consulting work is much lower than is generally supposed. In a recent analysis of empirical studies in the area, Boyer and Lewis note that many studies combine consulting income with other forms of supplemental income, such as that earned for teaching and research work, and thus overstate the extent and amount of consulting. Other studies overstate the extent of conflict with teaching and research obligations by failing to differentiate between academic year consulting and summer work for those faculty members on academic year appointments. Using recent data, Boyer and Lewis found that

> only 20.8 percent of the Ph.D. faculty in fields allied with science and engineering and only 12.4 percent of the Ph.D. faculty in the humanities devote some portion of their professional work time during the academic year to faculty consulting activities. . . . Moreover, of all Ph.D. faculty . . . only approximately 5 percent consult more than one day per week.[16]

They also found that, contrary to conventional wisdom, faculty members increased their consulting activities only slightly between 1975 and 1981—a period of financial stringency for many institutions and decline in "real dollar" faculty salaries.

Does paid consulting work really conflict with the fulfillment of teaching and research obligations? Are faculty members who consult less productive scholars and less committed teachers? Marsh and Dillon studied these questions in the somewhat larger context of faculty productivity and supplemental income. Using Ladd/Lipsett survey data and analyzing more than 3,000 responses from faculty members in doctoral institutions, comprehensive colleges and universities and liberal arts colleges, Marsh and Dillon correlated each of three income variables (base salary, percentage earned over base salary, and supplemental income) with each of a large number of productivity variables (e.g., number of books and articles, committee service, administrative assignments) correcting for academic rank, school type, discipline, and contract length. They found that supplemental income activities did not interfere with other activities. There was a strong, positive relationship between research productivity and all sources of supplemental income (including consulting income). This suggests that consulting activity does not impede, and may enhance, research and scholarly productivity. The relationships to departmental/institutional involvement were weaker, but this suggests that "consulting faculty are no less involved in service to their own institutions than are other faculty members." Teaching variables were negatively correlated with all income variables, suggesting that teaching is not rewarded in higher education, in either base salary or supplemental income.[17]

Does paid consulting work cause serious conflicts of interests for faculty members and institutions? Robert Linnel argues that it does:

> The entrepreneurial role is inconsistent with that of the full-time academic person. There is an intrinsic conflict-of-interest between the two roles, academic and entrepreneurial: the academic seeks knowledge and learning for its own sake whereas the entrepreneur seeks to use knowledge and learning for financial gain.[18]

Linell argues that there is a role for entrepreneurs in academe but not for those in full-time positions. He supports the public-service commitments of higher education and believes that colleges and universities should serve society by responding to needs for current, objective, and useful knowledge. He does not oppose technology transfer or industry-university relationships but argues that the paid relationship between the faculty member and an external organization subtly shifts the basis for deciding whether to participate in the activity away from criteria of academic benefits toward criteria of monetary and personal gain for the individual.[19]

Linnell defines the problem as one of inadequate salaries and contracts. He argues for full-time salaries competitive with external professional work and for calendar year appointments. He suggests that colleges and universities experiment with the establishment of professional practice plans—following medical school models—in areas such as business and engineering, as one means of paying for such an expensive change. The idea of professional practice plans tied to economic development activities is an intriguing idea that merits further study.[20]

Bok and others believe that less expensive measures can help prevent conflicts of interest with basic institutional and academic values. Carefully delineated policies and practices and intelligent arrangements in such areas as paid consulting, patent rights, intellectual property rights, and faculty and institutional participation in external business ventures can help minimize the risks of conflict.

It would seem, therefore, that colleges and universities should allow, even encourage, paid faculty consulting activity in areas related to local, regional, and national economic development. Building on existing faculty activities and areas of interest will enhance the institutional role in economic development programs. Furthermore, the linkages can enhance teaching by engaging students in real-world activities and enhance research by broadening definitions of problems and worthy subjects to study. To guard against conflicts of interest, however, colleges and universities should develop consulting policies that establish clear limits and ground rules.

Workload, reward systems, and provisions for faculty consulting raise important and difficult issues that must be addressed by colleges and universities serious about encouraging faculty involvement in economic development activities. In the end, they all relate to that composite of attitudes, beliefs, and expectations known as faculty morale. It is difficult to generalize about faculty morale, but institutional efforts to increase the level and quality of faculty economic development activity and to create an institutional response to societal needs in this area may well hinge on it. Bowen and Schuster voiced serious concern about the state of faculty morale on the college campuses, citing salaries and working conditions as contributing to low morale.[22] It is not easy to specify "how," but it is important for colleges and universities to demonstrate concern about their most vital resource.

Notes

[1]Harold E. Yuker, *Faculty Workload: Research, Theory, and Interpretation*, ASHE-ERIC Higher Education Research Report No. 10 (Washington, D.C.: Association for the Study of Higher Education, 1984).

[2]Howard R. Bowen and Jack H. Schuster, *American Professors: A National Resource Imperiled* (New York: Oxford University Press, 1986).

[3]Ernest A. Lynton and Sandra E. Elman, *Universities and the Knowledge Needs of Society* (forthcoming) (San Francisco: Jossey-Bass).

[4]John W. Creswell, *Faculty Research Performance: Lessons from the Sciences and the Social Sciences*, ASHE-ERIC Higher Education Research Report No. 4 (Washington, D.C.: Association for the Study of Higher Education, 1985), p. 24.

[5]John W. Creswell et al., "Enhancing Faculty Research Productivity," Paper presented at the annual meeting of the American Educational Research Association, New York, 1985, p. 40.

[6]Robert T. Blackburn et al., "Research Notes: Correlates of Faculty Publciations," *Sociology of Education*, 51:132-141.

[7]P. H. Crosson, *Public Service in Higher Education: Practices and Priorities*, ASHE-ERIC Higher Education Research Report No. 7 (Washington, D.C.: Association for the Study of Higher Education, 1983).

[8]Howard P. Tuckman, "The Academic Reward Structure in American Higher Education," in *Academic Rewards in Higher Education,* eds. Lewis and Becker (Ballinger, 1979).

[9]Lynton and Elman, p. 102.

[10]Sandra E. Elman and Sue Marx Smock, *Professional Service and Faculty Rewards: Toward an Integrated Structure* (Washington, D.C.: National Association of State Universities and Land-Grant Colleges, 1985), p. 15.

[11]Elman and Smock, p. 26.

[12]Ibid.

[13]Ibid.

[14]Ibid.

[15]Tuckman, p. 123.

[16]Carol M. Boyer and Darrell R. Lewis, "Faculty Consulting: Responsibility or Promiscuity?" *Journal of Higher Education,* 55(5):637-46.

[17]H. W. Marsh and K. E. Dillon, "Academic Productivity and Faculty Supplemental Income," *Journal of Higher Education,* 51:546-55.

[18]Robert H. Linnell, Ed., *Dollars and Scholars: An Inquiry into the Impact of Faculty Income Upon the Function and Future of the Academy* (Los Angeles: University of Southern California Press, 1982), p. 129.

[19]Ibid., p. 65.

[20]Ibid.

[21]Derek Bok, *Beyond the Ivory Tower: Social Responsibilities of the Modern University* (Cambridge: Harvard University Press, 1982).

[22]Bowen and Schuster.

16

University Management of Intellectual Property

Radford G. King

The author is director of the Office of Patent and Copyright Administration at the University of Southern California and executive director of the Western Research Application Center at the university.

Universities and colleges across the country currently face decisions about their role in economic development activities and about implementation of policies governing the management of intellectual property. This situation has arisen largely from the threat of reduced federal support for basic research, the possible reduction of indirect cost recovery rates, and increased pressure from federal, state and local governments to participate in job-creation activities.

Spurred by the threat of reduced government support for research, universities are now giving major attention to improving their industry relations and finding alternative sources of research funding. The literature abounds in articles on this increased activity: "The University/Industry Interface," "Business Universities Need Rules for Research Partnership," "Guidelines for Industry-Sponsored Research at Universities," "Corrupting Influence in Academia—Private Deals with Industry Undermine Trust in Universities," "Joint Venturing University Research: Negotiating Cooperative Agreements," "Research and Development Limited Partnership as a Device to Exploit University-Owned Technology," "Planting Seed Money in Campus Labs," "Universities Emerge as an Important Catalyst in the New Business Development Process," "High-tech Companies Court the College Connection," and "Research Universities Face New Fiscal Realities," to name a few.

Some universities have moved rapidly during the 1980s to form new research institutes or to restructure departments to make them more compatible with the needs of industry. At the same time, industry has shown a willingness to compromise its positions on academe. This cooperation between higher education and industry will continue, and the relative importance of industrial support will increase substantially.

New business ventures

At the same time, some universities are becoming quite entrepreneurial and creating their own "private" sources of research funding. Such programs stem largely from the current interest in high technology and its importance to the economic future of the country and from the perceived high return on venture investments. In most instances, the venture entity will receive exclusive rights to the intellectual property generated from funded research activity. New business entities will be formed to exploit the technology and to generate a return to the investors through equity participation and to the university through royalties.

Research and Development Limited Partnerships achieved considerable success during the early 1980s; over $3 billion was raised. Some funds have been successfully created to exploit university-owned technology. Implicit in these arrangements has been the acquisition of new technologies through research agreements with exclusive licensing clauses, or through licensing of technologies already developed. The next step toward commercialization is normally the formation of new business entities to manage the manufacturing and marketing of the products developed.

In addition to the above, a new type of professional has emerged who can be referred to as the "technology broker." This individual is normally a financial "finder," an attorney a patent agent, and/or a management consultant. His or her role is to identify a potentially commercial technology and faculty member(s), acquire an option to support research and license agreements, and package a financing program to implement the research.

Two different scenarios are emerging: the development of enhanced research relationships with industry (big business), and the development of alternative sources of research funding with the ultimate establishment of new businesses (small businesses).

During the past ten years it has been extensively reported that small business is the primary source of new job creation and that high-tech start-ups have the most likely chance of successful development. In a period of increasing unemployment, numerous states have taken steps to enhance the business environment for start-ups. Some states have created various forms of investments pools to encourage new technology development, others have become involved in supporting the development of research parks and/or enterprise zones, and considerable emphasis has been placed on the development of incubator programs.

Incubator facilities

As reported in the *Venture Capital Journal,* start-up companies in some areas are also discovering a haven in university "incubator" facilities. Although the incubators vary in terms of the general services they provide, the start-up company is offered low-cost space; access to a ready work force from the student population; faculty members skilled in advising on technical and managerial problems, and laboratory, library, computing, and office facilities.

Such facilities are located, for example, at Georgia Institute of Technology and Rensselaer Polytechnic Institute (RPI). RPI describes its incubator program as "the creation of an interactive environment between industry and education—where technological companies of tomorrow can develop and grow, honing their technical and entrepreneurial skills in an environment rich in the knowledge necessary to bring innovative ideas to the marketplace."

The University City Science Center in Philadelphia, a joint venture with twenty-three colleges and universities founded sixteen years ago, has one of the oldest incubator facilities. Pennsylvania's recently created Ben Franklin College Grant Program will help fund four additional incubator centers: one is being developed near Carnegie Mellon University and another at Lehigh University.

In 1978, the National Science Foundation (NSF) awarded a grant to the University of Utah to set up the Utah Innovation Center as a facility to house fledgling companies. When NSF funding was terminated in 1981, the program continued as a private enterprise that maintains close university ties.

Some universities have taken equity positions in companies started from technologies developed by their faculty. In some instances, faculty members, administrators, and trustees have also received equity positions in new entities. The university investments have usually come from the endowment funds of the institution.

New business start-ups

In addition to the activities of universities to support the development of new business, the federal government passed legislation to provide grants and contracts to small businesses as part of the research procurement activities of those federal agencies having research budgets our $100 million a year. The legislation is referred to as the Small Business Innovation Research (SBIR) Act. Although the SBIR excludes universities from eligibility for awards, many faculty members have established new small business entities that have received awards. In fact, some federal agency administrators have encouraged faculty members to make proposals under the SBIR program.

Although the primary activity of developing alternatives for research support has been directed to big business, universities are also becoming increasingly involved in new small business start-ups. In many instances, the motivation for new business creation has been the pressures of participating in the economic development activities of the state or region.

Universities have been involved in economic development activities for many years. Federally supported programs include the Small Business Administration—Small Business Development Centers, the Economic Development Administration—University Centers Program, the National Aeronautics and Space Administration—Industrial Application Centers, and the Department of Commerce—Trade Adjustment Assistance Centers. In addition, universities have programs in extension, continuing education, and special research, all designed to contribute to the economic viability of their communities. However, most of these programs have had justification in public service rather than in teaching or research.

The current environment of industry relations and new business start-ups relates chiefly to the generation of fiscal resources to maintain the research activities of institutions. This trend is heightening attention to the adequacy of the intellectual property management policies of most higher education institutions. Many universities are expanding their staffs to handle intellectual property matters. An indication of this expansion is reflected in the membership of the Society of University Patent Administrators (SUPA), which has grown from fifty-one founding members in 1975 to over 425 in 1986.

Intellectual property management

Intellectual property concerns patents, copyrights, trademarks, know-how, and tangible research results. The management of these assets is largely determined by the policies established by each institution and the resources budgeted to implement the policies.

Key policies are those pertaining to patents, copyrights, and conflicts of interest. These policies, when reviewed together, will normally define the position of the institution on title, disclosure, distribution of income, administrative responsibility and authority, and allowable activities of faculty and staff members and students that do not constitute conflicts of interest. Most universities are now either developing policy statements or revising existing ones.

Policies developed by each institution will indicate the extent to which the administration supports increased industry relations, development of new business enterprises, and other economic development activities. Some primary areas of concern are identified below.

Publication rights

The right to publish arises from the fundamental purpose of a university—to preserve and transmit existing knowledge and to generate new knowledge. As the primary trustee of the world's knowledge, the university has an obligation to society, and the ability to fulfill that obligation depends on the university's freedom to publish. Most university/industry agreements clearly spell out the retention of the right to publish; however, because industrial sponsors frequently have proprietary interests to protect, they will ask the university to keep confidential any proprietary information it acquires from the sponsor to conduct the research. This conflict is usually resolved by allowing the sponsor a limited time, such as thirty days, to review proposed publications to determine whether confidential information is included. In some instances it may be necessary to provide for a delay of publication to allow the sponsor or the university to prepare and file patent applications if patentable material was included in the document. A delay of ninety days would not be unreasonable.

Universities normally will not deal in trade secrets although this practice is common in industry. However, when substantial investments in the research may yield substantial returns, it is not unusual for the sponsor to request secrecy agreements from research staff personnel working on a project. This is usually accomplished as a condition of employment and is normally unacceptable to an academic institution. The resolution of this matter will require considerable justification and definition as an exception to policy.

Licensing and patents

Title to inventions is normally vested in the university through an employment condition to assign rights, subject only to sponsor agreements. Rights to inventions sponsored by government funds were somewhat confusing prior to the implementation of Public Law 96-517, which became effective July 1, 1981. The law effectively gave small business and nonprofit contractors the "first right of refusal" to patent rights covering inventions conceived or, in patents language, "reduced to practice" under a government research contract. Uniform standards were set for all government agencies (except the Tennessee Valley Authority), replacing the complex and often confusing web of regulations previously established by each individual agency. Even with the clarification of rights under government sponsorship, title issues may often be complex. It is not unusual for coinventorship to occur between faculty members from different institutions working together on the same project. Because patent policies at most universities are similar, resolution of coinventorship is usually resolved by a management agreement between the two parties. Many times this agreement is determined after the invention is created. However, it is critical to define title rights in industry agreements, especially when industry personnel work side by side with faculty members, because patent policies at most industrial firms are quite different, especially in their provisions for the sharing of royalty income with inventors.

As more faculty members become involved in equity positions in new business ventures, it is important to determine whether a faculty member had title to the technology prior to the formation of the business entity. This issue becomes even more confusing when one considers that an SBIR award, venture capital support, or an incubator project may be based on a technology conceived and/or developed at a university and under either government or industry sponsorship wherein the faculty member does not have title to the technology.

Liability and risk management

As universities become more involved in patent licensing, adequate risk management becomes of increasing concern because of product liability issues. Although universities as licensors have not been held responsible for the actions of licensees, potential judgment against a university, especially under the "deep pockets" concept, poses a real threat.

Typically, university research results are transferred to a licensee at a very early stage of development, and the final product sent to the market place has undergone considerable modification. In these instances, the university licensor has not been held to be in the "stream of distribution"; however, a licensor of a product technology that is virtually the same as the product ultimately marketed may considered to be in the stream of distribution and subject to judgment actions. This problem is compounded when one considers that many software products, new materials, or chemical formulas may be marketed virtually in the same form transferred to the licensee.

This concern has not only increased the need for comprehensive, negative warrant and indemnification clauses but in many cases will require substantial insurance coverage clauses. Because product liability insurance may not be available to the licensee or is prohibitively expensive, the university may assess the financial condition of the licensee to determine whether the risk/return relationship is adequate. Many small firms will not qualify under a conservative approach to risk management.

As the issues of risk management are identified, concern grows about the need for distribution agreements to exchange or transfer new technologies to other academic research institutions. Even questions about the risk of exposure of publications have been raised. Until these issues are clearly resolved, each institution must make business decisions that have significant implications for the conduct of research relations with industry and espcially the development of entrepreneurial ventures.

Institutional policy issues

Determining conflict-of-interest policies in today's environment is critical. Policies must address such issues as consulting activities, equity participation in business ventures, accepting research financed by firms in which faculty members have equity interests, licensing intellectual property rights to firms wherein the inventor-faculty member is also an equity holder in the licensee, clear definition of responsibility for resolution of conflict-of-interest issues, and definition of disclosure requirements by faculty members.

In addition, policy statements should clearly define the university's position on investing in firms in which faculty members are major stockholders and on whether the university may establish for-profit subsidiaries to manufacture products that compete with products made by industry.

After establishing clearly defined policy positions, it is important to establish means for disseminating the information and educating the institution's administrators and faculty and staff members about its implementation. Development of handouts for industrial partners, venture capitalists, technology brokers, and representatives of federal, state, and local governments can be critical to the adequate control of the relationship.

Clearly defined organizational structures within the institutions, including designation of responsibility and authority, should be developed. Historically, universities have had many different models for intellectual property management. Responsibility may be allocated to a contracts and grants office; an office of patent, trademark, and copyright administration; a director of research; an office of business affairs; a development office; or any combination thereof. Clear-cut goals and objectives should be established and methods for evaluation of performance decided.

There is considerable disagreement on what the proper role of higher education institutions should be as it relates to technology transfer and involvement in economic development activities. In the coming years many models will evolve, none of which will constitute an ideal model for all institutions.

American universities collectively represent the most sophisticated research resource in the world. Most people accept the idea that the results of that research should be made available for commercial application. A variety of reasons are offered in support, many of them carrying an urgency arising from the circumstances of our time. The health of our industrial base and our international competitive position calls for as much ingenuity as we can muster. Concern for the health of our people and our environment demands that ideas that serve those needs be put to use. The relative decline in government funding, along with the rise in the cost of research, create a need on the part of universities for new sources of research support. The still dominant role government funding plays in the support of university research, however, demands that the public benefit from the research. The commercial exploitation of university-owned technology to obtain such funds is not only proper but is encouraged by the federal government.

While acknowledging that univeristies must do better in making their research results available for commercial purposes, their leadership has shown proper caution in avoiding commercial entanglement which would compromise academic values. The quest for profit cannot be allowed to shape the university research agenda or influence the faculty appointment process. The needs of commercial users of university research for secrecy must yield to the academic imperative of openness. The university must ensure that the technology it makes available to others for profit is used responsibly, and that its service to the goals above is defined. At the same time, the university must ensure that its name and reputation do not become commercial coin. This is a point of more than mere priggishness, and more than a ploy to avoid product liability. The commercialization of the university's reputation would erode the authority of its scholars as objective commentators as gravely as would its politicization.

17

Linking Universities with Communities: The Cleveland Experience

John A. Flower

The author is provost and vice president for academic affairs at Cleveland State University (OH).

Cleveland, the largest urban area in Ohio (the nation's most urbanized state), is making a turn-around in economic vitality. Its population is diminished, and many of its jobs are gone, but new partnerships have been forged that are revitalizing the city in many ways. A key partner in Cleveland's regeneration is Cleveland State University, which, in concert with a state-supported initiative involving all eight of Ohio's urban universities, is building local capabilities.

Cleveland State is located just eighteen blocks from Cleveland's recognized center, Public Square, and is unquestionably an "urban" university. Indeed, its urban mission was clearly outlined in the documents of its founding in 1964, by act of the Ohio General Assembly. Though the phrase "economic development" was not as prominent in 1964 as it is today, the new university's mandate "to provide high-quality, easily accessible higher education opportunities to residents of the Cleveland metropolitan region" was clearly an economic development strategy. By establishing the College of Urban Affairs in 1977, Cleveland State clearly demonstrated its intent to fulfill its urban mission.

An urban demonstration program

Cleveland State University's ability to forge community linkages has been considerably expedited by the Ohio Urban Demonstration Program administered by the Ohio Board of Regents. With primary leadership from Cleveland State, Ohio took the lead among the states in 1979 in providing state support to encourage university-community partnerships. The Ohio General Assembly established and appropriated $1 million for the first two years of the program, with an increase to $2.3 millin for the 1986-87 biennium. The state funds have been leveraged by the participating universities at a rate of nearly three to one through the financial support of local governments, private foundations, state and federal agencies, and private industry.

Federal government assistance has been but a promise for urban university programs. Indeed, Ohio's Urban University Program was developed as part of strategy to "capture" promised dollars from the 1980 Title XI amendment of the Higher Education Act of 1965. But funds were never authorized for Title XI, and the National Urban Grant University Program has remained a pipe dream.

In this era of federal budget cuts, urban universities have an unparalleled opportunity to catalyze the forging of local partnerships.

Economic recovery for Cleveland, and for other industrial cities in the Northeast and Midwest, clearly depends on self-directed local and state actions rather than additional major infusions of federal funds. Thus, universities located in such cities can be instrumental in building the capacity of people and of institutions and organizations to govern, to provide better services with less money, to make decisions based on accurate, up-to-date information, and to understand the implications of economic, demographic, social, and technological forces. Much of this can be assumed an *educational* role, to be sure, but Cleveland State is privileged to incorporate that capacity building into its *research* and *public-service* missions as well.

In funding the Urban University Program, the board of regents determined that initial state funding could support one major "prototype" urban center and established it at Cleveland State University in recognition of the critical problems facing the city. Housed within the College of Urban Affairs, the Urban Center is committed to developing a better understanding of the problems facing Cleveland and similar urban areas.

Spawned in a period of urgency and given a broad mission, the university and the College of Urban Affairs and its urban center had to "focus"—to plan a manageable set of functions to control expectations of being "all things to all people." Today, the university's programs are concentrated in three areas: (1) urban policy analysis and research, (2) urban public management (including public finance and budget), and (3) urban planning, design, and development.

The Urban Center at Cleveland State's College of Urban Affairs employs thirty professionals engaged in most aspects of urban affairs but emphasizing public finance, housing research, neighborhood development, and economic development. The Urban Center produces basic and applied research, provides technical assistance, and conducts training classes. Working relationships have been developed with more than 130 organizations in greater Cleveland, ranging from City of Cleveland municipal departments to businesses and neighborhood groups. The range of services provided by the Urban Center is indeed broad.

Meeting diverse needs

Following is a sampling of successful and significant activities emanating from Cleveland State.

■ One of its highest-profile services puts the capabilities of the university's mainframe computer to work on public issues through the Northern Ohio Data & Information Service (NODIS). Serving as a data clearinghouse for the region, it maintains a data base of 1980 U.S. Census, housing, economic, and geographic information. As one of three regional data information centers in the state and as a Census Bureau affiliate, it is the primary source in northern Ohio for urban data.

■ The ability of NODIS to provide information, from a quick fact over the phone to a detailed demographic profile of a specific area, has produced more than 2,500 customers, ranging from local governments to businesses.

■ Public finance is the specialty of the Fiscal Futures Service, which conducts basic and applied research on state and local government spending, revenue sources, and budgeting practices. The service is also cooperating with Bowling Green State University to produce detailed economic forecasts that will assist finance directors in projecting tax revenues. The Fiscal Futures Service publishes a newsletter on fiscal matters for public finance officials and a quarterly magazine covering the economy of the state and its major cities and development issues.

■ The Urban Center's economic development program ranges from research on the existing local strengths cities should use to seek new development to building a computerized data base of economic information for use by researchers and developers.

■ The Housing Policy Research Project studies computerized records of home sales in Cuyahoga County to produce information on mortgage lending patterns and housing demand and supply, and to track the subtle patterns of housing discrimination. A report on home appreciation in the county from 1976 to 1984 and an annual report on home-buying trends in Cleveland are valuable resources for realtors, bankers, and local government officials.

■ The Center for Neighborhood Development (a division of the Urban Center) offers invaluable technical assistance to neighborhood and community groups. A case in point is a neighborhood-based crime prevention program that has just secured over $250,000 from four sources. Center staff met with twelve neighborhood organizations in August 1984 to discuss the Cleveland Bar Association's Task Force Report on Violent Crime. Those twelve groups formed the Cleveland Neighborhood Safety Coalition, which received technical assistance from Urban Center personnel in researching existing neighborhood safety programs, preparing a concept paper for fund development use, and contacting potential funders. The $250,000 raised (from the City of Cleveland, the State of Ohio, and the Cleveland and Gund Foundations) will support full-time safety coordinators in each of the twelve participating organizations, an overall project coordinator, a revolving loan fund for the home security program, and program overhead. Expansion of the program to other neighborhoods is anticipated. Everyone involved is acutely aware of the importance of crime prevention programs to an area's economic well-being, and such a university-community project can be expected to have noticeable "ripple effect."

■ The Urban Center also conducts training programs to enhance the leadership capacity of public officials. In cooperation with Case Western Reserve University and the Ohio Department of Administrative Services, the Urban Center conducts a two-week training program for top-level state cabinet officers. This "Ohio Executive Institute" stresses leadership skills. Last January, the Urban Center conducted its third annual seminar for council members from Cuyahoga County suburbs on consensus-building strategies for use in budget-cutting sessions.

In addition to the extensive Urban Center activities within the city and the region, other Cleveland State University initiatives exemplify university-community partnerships.

The Fenn College of Engineering at Cleveland State is one the three academic "partners" in the Cleveland Advanced Manufacturing Program (CAMP). The Advanced Manufacturing Center at Cleveland State is developing general expertise and strengthening research capabilities in four areas:

■ computer-aided design and manufacturing,
■ in-process sensing and control,
■ integrated manufacturing systems,
■ man-machine interface.

Ohio companies can turn to the Advanced Manufacturing Center for applied research and information.

The CAMP program is part of the statewide Thomas Alva Edison Program, approved by the Ohio legislature in 1983 to stimulate technology innovation and enterprise in Ohio by providing start-up funding to accademic/business partnerships. There are six Edison technology centers throughout the state. The Cleveland center emphasizes integrated manufacturing. The other centers focus on technologies in which Ohio holds world leadership positions, such as welding, polymers, animal genetics, and date-base management. The public will hear more about successful university-community partnerships as these programs become fully operational.

Smaller-scale but similarly ambitious efforts are supported by the Urban University Program at the seven other Ohio urban universities. Collectively, in a single biennium (1984-85), the eighteen institutions produced these accomplishments:

■ More than 250 faculty members and students were involved in research on urban problems, requested by community groups;

■ More than 150 research reports, papers, and publications on every aspect of urban affairs were published;

■ More than 3,000 people received training through workshops, seminars, and conferences on dealing with urban concerns.

Issues and implications

Additional evidence for the effect of universities on economic development appeared recently when academic units of the university competed for a new funding source, "Academic Challenge Grants." In order to qualify for this new infusion of state money, academic departments presented proposals containing statements that described the proposed program's potential impact on strategic statewide needs, with emphasis on issues in economic revitalization of Ohio. As a musician, the author was gratified to see that augmentation of the Music Composition Program at Cleveland State is expected to have a direct economic impact. That proposal states,

Cleveland is especially renowned as an international center of
excellence in music. In addition to contributing to the quality of
life in the region, this resource contributes to the ability of the
city to retain and attract businesses that depend on the availability of highly educated personnel.

The statement captures the intricacy and importance of universities in local economic development. The opportunities for universities to contribute in this arena are boundless.

Sometimes the word *opportunity* is used (by optimists, in particular) as a euphemism for "problem." But whether seen as opportunities, problems, or challenges, the issues affecting university-community partnerships include the following.

The *funding* for university-community partnerships is perhaps the most critical issue of all. William C. Pendleton, program officer for the Ford Foundation, who headed extensive efforts in the 1960s to develop university-city linkages, has summed up the two essential ingredients for successful urban centers:

hard funding and good leadership. In Ohio "hard funding" has been secured and used to match funds supplied by public and private entities involved with the universities in cooperative economic development projects. But future financial support for these initiatives is uncertain. With federal funding policy changes, the Urban University Program in Ohio will face close scrutiny in the competition for state support. Moreover, the "good leadership" component that Pendleton emphasizes is expensive to provide: job announcements typically state "compensation commensurate with experience," but it is not always possible financially to hire someone with the degree of experience needed.

This year Congress may even eliminate the dream of Title XI. The entire Higher Education Act is up for renewal. While the House version, H.R. 37000, retains Title XI—and adds a part called "The National Higher Education and Economic Development Program"—there is support for stripping the Higher Education Act of those programs that have not been funded in the past—Title XI among them. The big question remains: how will university-community linkages be funded?

For the university, another critical issue is that of "intellectual merit." Do institutional partnerships with the community result in the generation of new knowledge? Will the age-old discussions on the relative merits of applied vs. basic research cease or become louder?

Another issue is how much *change* will be forced on the university. Some writers have said that universities are among the most unchanged institutions in the world. It seems that university-community relationships will require some significant changes on the part of the university. Project control may be manageable on a project-by-project basis, but much more difficult when substantial funding of a major commitment comes from outside the university. Ownership issues are surfacing more frequently now that university personnel have more opportunity to participate in product design and development. Long-standing academic regulations on consulting time, on patent and copyright ownership, and on royalties are being challenged by faculty researchers. Universities that have had unwritten expectations have had to move quickly to codify those expectations.

A fourth issue concerns the "distortion of effort" that may result from university-community linkages. When many more opportunities for financial support through cooperative projects fall into engineering and the sciences than into the humanities departments, university officials are hard pressed to allocate support dollars equitably. In a period of shrinking resources, it would be all too easy to tie the university allocation to external fund generation in some way. There is a danger that such a step would destroy "incentive" no matter who was involved. Any department might "slow down" in its proposal generation rather than risk loss of university funding, thus eliminating at the outset some extremely valuable cooperative ventures.

The final issue relates to the *positioning* of partnerships within the university. Will they become widespread, linked to every academic unit? Or will they tend to cluster in defined "centers," such as the Urban Center at Cleveland State? Is one model better than the other? What issues are concomitant to this "position"? Cleveland State is facing new issues such as "How is pay equity influenced by the introduction of 'market conditions,'" and "Can we charge our community partners the full costs of research?"

Universities can make substantial contributions to the better understanding and improved analysis of the issues and choices facing urban areas. That capability, however, is not limited to urban universities; town/gown relationships are significant for all universities.

Cleveland has laid a strong foundation for establishing linkages that are resulting in both productive communication and cooperation. The university takes great pride in contributing to the economic well-being of a great city. All universities should forge such links at the earliest opportunity.

Appendix

National Project on Higher Education and Economic Development

Advisory Committee

Johnnie Albertson, Deputy Associate Administrator for Business Development, Small Business Administration

Carol Eliason, Education Analyst and Consultant

Louis Bone, Director, Economic Development Technical Assistance Center, Benedict College (SC)

Candice Brisson, Staff Associate for Research and Programs, Southern Growth Policies Board

Larry Crockett, Director, Special Projects Division, University of Michigan

William E. Davis, Chancellor, Oregon State System of Higher Education

James Hefner, President, Jackson State University (MS)

George Johnson, President, George Mason University (VA)

James King, Director, Small Business Development Centers, State University of New York

Radford King, Director, Western Research Application Center, University of Southern California

Alan Magazine, President, Council on Competitiveness

H. Leroy Marlow, Director, Pennsylvania Technical Assistance Program, Pennsylvania State University

William McCarthy, Policy Analyst, National League of Cities

Beverly Milkman, Director, Office of Planning, Technical Assistance, Research and Evaluation, Economic Development Administration

Rudy Oswald, Director of Research, AFL/CIO

Gail Parkinson, Director, Regional Economic Assistance Center, School of Management, State University of New York at Buffalo

Eugene Stark, Industrial Initiatives Officer, Los Alamos National Laboratory

David Swanson, Director, Center for Industrial Research and Service, Iowa State University

Robert Swanson, Chancellor, University of Wisconsin-Stout

Project Staff

Helen Roberts, Director, Office of Community Development and Public Service, American Association of State Colleges and Universities

Karen Henderson, Program Associate, Office of Community Development and Public Service, American Association of State Colleges and Universities

Deborah White-Skelton, Senior Administrative Assistance, Office of Community Development and Public Service, American Association of State Colleges and Universities

Harold Williams, Washington Representative, National Association of Management and Technical Assistance Centers

Tom Chmura, Senior Policy Analyst, Public Policy Center, SRI International

AASCU Task Force on Economic Development

Robert S. Swanson (*Chair*), Chancellor, University of Wisconsin-Stout

David E. Gilbert (*Vice Chair*), President, Eastern Oregon State College

Steven Altman, President, Texas A&I University

Saul K. Fenster, President, New Jersey Institute of Technology

James A. Hefner, President, Jackson State University

Rod C. Kelchner, President, Mansfield University of Pennsylvania

William C. Merwin, President, Northern Montana College

W. Edmund Moomaw, Chancellor, Clinch Valley College (WV)

Helen Popovich, President, Florida Atlantic University

Ed D. Roach, President, West Texas State University

Olin Sansbury, Chancellor, University of South Carolina at Spartanburg

Robert A. Scott, President, Ramapo College of New Jersey

Thomas M. Stauffer, Chancellor, University of Houston-Clear Lake

Walter B. Waetjen, President, Cleveland State University

John P. Watkins, President, California University of Pennsylvania

Chia-Wei Woo, President, San Francisco State University (CA)

Betty Lentz Siegel, President, Kennesaw College (GA)

Patricia F. Sullivan (*Staff Liaison*), Program Associate, Office of Governmental Relations, American Association of State Colleges and Universities